Sally,

Thanks for all of
you help and
guidance.

Lynn
EPNPS
01/05/02

"This is truly a 'novel' in the sense that it represents an entirely **new** approach to story-telling. Never before has history been recounted by a Tree; and no ordinary tree, but an aged and venerable yewess, the Matriarch of the forest and an Archetype of treeness in her own right. As a forester and a conservationist I believe this book is a landmark, it combines hard science with romantic fiction in a way that is always accurate and informative but **never** dull. It puts a single yew tree centre stage and by doing so, forces the reader to identify with her and with all trees."

—Jean-Paul Jeanrenaud, Head of the Forest Programme at WWF International Secretariat.

"The Story of Yew will sow seeds for a rising generation who will be more environmentally responsible than ours and inspire all who care about the countryside to fight for a better rural heritage for future generations. I wish this book all the success it deserves."

—The late Phil Drabble , naturalist, author and TV personality.

"I have read *The Story of Yew* thoroughly and critically and with much pleasure. It is informative, entertaining, and has a refreshing approach to some ancient and modern beliefs. Temperamentally unattracted to whimsy and elaborate writing, I nevertheless found this highly imaginative tale so firmly grounded in fact and unassailable scientifically, that, far from being put off, I found this work a pleasing read.

"Since I had been consulted on the botany involved and on the physiology, health and growth of this extraordinary species, I was particularly attentive to the passages relevant to these subjects. They passed the test triumphantly.

"As a blend of science and imaginative fiction, this is a remarkable book, far removed from 'science-fiction' as normally understood. It deals with the real world in an inventive way without putting a foot wrong."

—The late Alan Mitchell VMH, leading authority on trees of the Northern Hemisphere, founder of the Tree Register, and author of *Trees of Britain and Northern Europe, The Garden Tree*, etc.

"I have enjoyed reading *The Story of Yew*. Although I read a lot about plants and natural history in general, I can safely say that I have never read anything quite like your novel before. It is the originality of your approach that impresses me most."

—Stephen Blackmore, Associate Director at The Natural History Museum, now Regius Keeper of the Royal Botanic Garden Edinburgh.

"I found *The Story of Yew* a pleasurable and refreshing experience. One of the surprising aspects of the work was the author's ability to maintain interest from beginning to end. Only a supreme optimist would have attempted to write a novel with this title, but the end result is a work of great charm. [...] The blending of the scientific with the fictional was skillfully accomplished. The fiction of St. Patrick vanishing the snakes from Iceland, the sojourn of Aenas in Hibernia, the absence of woodpeckers could only be matched by a vivid Celtic imagination"
—The late Alan Brady, Director of the National Botanic Gardens at Glasnevin, Dublin, Ireland.

"We found *The Story of Yew* an exceptionally well constructed, original, captivating story. Without doubt it will be of the greatest help in raising an awareness of the magic of trees in young and old alike."
—Robert Osborne, Director of The Tree Council.

"*The Story of Yew* has achieved a combination of history, botany and philosophy in a most unusual manner. The ITF wishes you every success."
—John Caunce, Chairman of the International Tree Foundation.

"*The Story of Yew* was read with great interest and enjoyment. Being written from the Yew's own viewpoint is excellent and gives the reader a very welcome and much needed reflection on mankind. I hope that many readers of this novel will begin to see that we humans are but a mere fraction of the Earth's wondrous ecology."
—Martin Blunt, for Tree Spirit.

The Story of Yew

Guido Mina di Sospiro

FINDHORN
Press

First published by Findhorn Press in 2001

ISBN 1-899171-63-0

British Library Cataloguing-in-Publication Data.
A catalogue record for this book is available from the British Library.

Library of Congress Catalog Card Number: 00-109404

Cover and inside illustrations © Ernesto Pescini 2001
Photographs of author and Muckross Abbey Yew by Stenie

Edited by Tony Mitton
Layout by Pam Bochel
Cover design by Thierry Bogliolo

Printed and bound by WS Bookwell, Finland

Published by
Findhorn Press

The Park, Findhorn
Forres IV36 3TY
Scotland
Tel 01309 690582
Fax 01309 690036

P.O. Box 13939
Tallahassee
Florida 32317-3939, USA
Tel 850 893 2920
Fax 850 893 3442

e-mail info@findhornpress.com
findhornpress.com

In loving memory of Andrea

FOREWORD

The Story of Yew *is just that—the story of a yew tree. A two thousand-year-old specimen relates its memoirs for the benefit of the human race. The narrative is in the first person simply because the storyteller is the yew itself.*

Only by lending an unbiased ear can one appreciate the words spoken by the yew tree. It follows that the kind listeners should put aside their assumptions on the superiority of the human race.

How I chanced upon this age-old testimony, and then transcribed it, is inessential.

Legend has it that before the construction of the heaven-reaching tower of Babel there was but one language. The yew has overcome the communication barrier between humans and trees by employing a shared language. We live on common ground.

ONE

Twenty-four thousand seven hundred and forty moons ago: I remember... being born. I remember sprouting slowly from the soft Earth, and receiving mother's greetings, still so close to the ground, and yet already gazing up with my first leaflets...

...It had been drizzling for days and nights. Sometimes it had been raining pelting, driving rain, the type of downpours we seedlings all feared, for it could easily snatch us off the ground. To be uprooted when there were practically no roots yet! But then the harsh rain had abated, and turned into the welcoming drizzle which was caressing my brothers, sisters and me. Mother looked down towards us, lovingly, hoping that we would finally grow out of Mother Earth.

It had been a long time since we had dropped to the ground wrapped in the pulpy flesh of a berry. It was then the end of summer, yet I recall an unseasonable warmth. So warm was it during the day and lukewarm at night that we were forced to ripen and fall ahead of time.

Most of us left by ways of the sky, swallowed by birds. These could digest only the berry, and eventually delivered the seeds here and there, where chance would have it. Others, like myself, were left to a wingless flight, sometimes lengthened by a gust of wind, but more often undisturbed by anything other than the pull of Mother Earth.

About Her I have already spent a few kind words, which by no means do I intend to take back. "Soft Earth", however, is a compliment indeed. When I landed on it, it felt more like *crashing* against it. True, I dropped from one of mother's highest branches.

I remember... being born.

Also true, I had grown rather plump and... heavy, owing to the uncharacteristic warmth and mother's nourishing sap. But a bang like the one I experienced on impact, *that* I did not expect. I had fallen on virtually bare rock, neither soft, nor warm, nor rich in elements essential to my growth.

With the coming of winter, I went to sleep, thinking about mother and her tender care. I thought about her all the time, though slightly, so as not to offend my new, sterner Mother.

Winter saw to it. And so did the wind. And the leaves of many a neighbouring tree. An orchestrated effort. I know now that it was she, Mother Nature herself, who saw to it.

A myriad leaves turned colour and fell from the trees in the forest. Not from mother or other yews, though, for we are evergreen and do not change leaves by dropping them all at once. Rather, from grand oaks, slender birches, and many other trees. Then the wind scattered and piled them here and there, seemingly at random. Some of them, or perhaps many, I can't tell—I was slumbering—covered me like a warm blanket. In time, white powdery crystals came down from the sky. Not much, but enough to fasten the leaves on the ground.

When spring was sprung, the snow melted into countless rivulets, and the sodden leaves began to decay. Slowly, at first, for it was still quite nippy.

I was to sprout amid leaf mould, a rich surrogate Mother Earth had provided for me instead of the stark rock. Very little depth to it, but enough to sustain the initial growth, the most crucial phase in the life of any tree.

And so I sprouted, slowly, cautiously, beneath a crescent moon and a warm-hearted sun. Not too warm, I must own, and frequently darkened by clouds laden with rain. But these were welcome too, each ingredient contributing to the recipe of Mother Nature's Kitchen. And mother caressed me with her gazes, along with my brothers and sisters, all hatching, sprouting during these eventful days.

My memory was all there, already. It had been there even whilst I was taking shape among mother's branches. But it was blurred, or perhaps dazed by the wonder of birth. The only thing I could make out distinctly was a feeling of uneasiness, one presumably caused by my own growth. The sky was pulling me upwards, and my fragile stem was growing as straight up as my strength would allow. Conversely, I was experiencing a strong pull downwards. My first rootlet, the underground equivalent of my stem, was supposed to go straight down through the earth. But how could I pierce solid rock? If I was alive it was thanks to the leaf mould and the little soil to be found in it. By then I had gone through it, and now what?

Well, I can state in retrospect that nothing is quite that fixed in nature. By my birthplace there was a gentle incline. Some of my rootlets went up the slope, by which I mean in the same general direction of the stem, not quite as straight up, but up anyway. In time, I would grow stronger, and, in all hopefulness, my roots would be able to burrow into the limestone crevices. Meanwhile, I could grow outwardly. My stem, my trunk-to-be, might not grow quite as high as it was meant to, but thicker, stouter. Tiny as I was, I keenly knew that I was already in love with Mother Nature's Kitchen. Why should I give everything up just out of strict adherence to a North-South principle?

Being alive was delightful. I could sense that having made it thus far was the outset of a triumphant life. Why, it must be! I wish you could have been gazing round as I was, all smells and sights, all enchantment. My two mothers; the leaves, and the grasses, and the leaves of grass between streams, lakes and clouds; the blooms brought about by springtide; the many seedlings as young and hopeful as I was; the salmon and trout in the waters; the foxes and stags on the ground; the robins and chaffinches in the air... The world spun round, and I kept drinking the rain, growing on the earth, harvesting the sun.

It was not merely an auspicious beginning. I knew then as I know now after the test of time that life, with all its attributes, with all my attributes, was well worth living. There was great promise in it, I could somehow recognise, and Mother Nature's Kitchen was bound to be a marvellous playground. As long as I learnt not to take and partake in excess, life would unfold gloriously, and open before me like a treasure house full of secrets.

TWO

As warmer breezes started to waft through the woods, and brighter sun rays to lighten our northern sky, springtide alighted like stardust, and I began to grow apace. At a slow pace, that is, oh, so imperceptibly slow!

I remember staring at mother, at other yews, at the oaks and many more giants all towering over me. And I remember something close to feeling their roots all over, everywhere. Some birch and alder seedlings, tiny things like me, were growing ever so quickly, leaf after leaf. They were mothered by the frequent rains and, I thought, by the sight of many intermittent rainbows too. And I, so little, so small... Good grief, was I going to live my life as some sort of dwarf? That was a depressing prospect, though I know now that dwarf variations of otherwise sizeable plants are appreciated as curiosities by plant collectors.

I asked my ever-present memory: "Am I normal?"

"What do you mean by 'normal'?"

Goodness gracious, I don't recall liking this answer. In fact, I rather disliked it and, disheartened, turned to the life-giver, my mother, for a more caring insight.

Luckily enough, no, I was not a dwarf, and was meant to grow and attain, in time, great size. In time, precisely. But when? How was I to know, then, that a key to longevity is keeping a low profile? How was I to know that those very seedlings I envied—the birch and alder ones—were growing so swiftly, almost hastily, so as to take full advantage of a short life?

How was I to know so many things, back then, a miniature of a tree, no trunk to be spoken of yet, but a wigwagging stem, much like a flower's, and a few leaflets? Was I supposed to try and sort things out through my built-in memory? What if it continued to play tricks on me, rather than supplying me with straight answers? Perhaps it was blurred forever. Perhaps it was coming into focus by giving me befogging answers. I had better leave it alone for a while, and seek the answers elsewhere. From my two mothers, for instance. Mother spoke straightforwardly, but Mother Nature did not. She used go-betweens.

The first I remember was a krikiting oddity. This little thing—it was little indeed, for I barely reached knee-height then, and yet I could already look down towards it—introduced itself as the Knowing Cricket. At first, his words, it was a he, sounded like a rasping "krit-it, krit-it," but, as I paid more attention, I managed to understand them.

I had never heard a cricket talk, or even heard of a talking cricket, but then, wasn't I ridiculously young? This chirping thing was telling me that he came from another planet, and that he was very, very old, older than I could imagine.

"Somehow," he said, "I'm bent on talking to trees. No matter how big, they never squash me, unless they drop something, say, a cone, or a dried-up branch." Consequently, he liked saplings and seedlings best of all.

He was, as he put it, "the wisest and oldest cricket in the Land," and knew all the secrets of the animals. He understood them for he spoke their language. Indeed, he was fluent in all languages, but I did not quite grasp that at the time. Now, he might have been as old, knowledgeable, and extraterrestrial as he claimed, but was it wise to be so boastful?

"I know most things. I have seen it all."

As the birds stood silent and everything appeared to come to a halt in the otherwise jabbering forest, I became mesmerised by his clicking voice, and asked him to tell me everything I should know. Although I could still not make out most of what I saw and heard, I suppose I was able to perceive his good intentions. This was a relief, for I already feared... fear.

"Don't worry, my little friend, and don't fear. You see, as children easily tremble and feel afraid at the unseen terrors of darkness," and surely the nights were eerie, with creepers and critters, and whispers and cries beneath the stars, "so at times the wisest amongst us have fear, in broad daylight, of things which we really shouldn't dread any more than those fancies children like you tremble at in the dark."

"Do you mean, there's nothing to fear?"

"No, not really, my little one. I must confess that the older I get, the more I fear that I might end in some animal's gut. Or that a charging boar or leaping stag might squash me. What a pity that would be, after so many, many years, to die like that. But listen: fear can and must be controlled, lest you should have a miserable life. Look over there, by the lake shore. Can you see the jackdaw and the trout? Listen to what they're saying."

I did as told.

"Hello, Brownie," the bird said to the fish, which was a brown trout, and therefore he called her Brownie, "what are you doing here on the grass? Digging for worms?"

"It was a fly," the trout answered. "I jumped too high for him, and here I am, stranded. If I don't get back into the water very soon I'll be out for good, because I'm nearly stupefied."

"You ought to stick to worms and leave the flies to the swallows, Brownie."

"Now," the Knowing Cricket interjected, "to resume our conversation—"

"—But what about Brownie, poor thing?"

"Who? Whom did you say?"

"Brownie, the trout."

"Oh, the trout. Well, isn't it sweet, when stormy winds assail the waters, safe on the shore to watch another's distress? Not that it is joy to view another's affliction, but it *is* sweet to know yourself free from that sea of troubles, isn't it?"

It seemed to me that the Knowing Cricket was getting things mixed up. For one thing, the trout was in trouble precisely because she was on the shore and out of the water. And, apart from that, I felt terrible about it. Something must be done, and I wished *I* could do something to save Brownie.

Eventually, the jackdaw said: "Come on, Brownie, I'll have you back where you belong in no time."

The bird caught the trout's tail in his beak and flung her into the lake with a snappy twist of his neck. Just in time, for the wretch had reached her last gasp.

That was sweeter by far, I thought. To be safe was sweet. But to watch someone in distress was bitter indeed, and, "You know," I told the Cricket, "the sweetest thing of them all is for everybody to be safe and happy."

"Mm," he commented, his long hind legs rasping together, "a noble soul, apparently. Or just a candid soul? The fly must be most happy about his narrow escape, wouldn't you agree? And worms dislike both jackdaws and trout." He leant forward, waving his antennæ. "You must learn to recognise friend and foe, and the sooner the better."

"Why?"

"So that you may avoid trouble and live a long life."

That made sense, though I still did not know what he meant by keeping out of trouble. I could not fly, or swim, or run away from danger. As I was about to ask him exactly how I could steer away from trouble, the Knowing Cricket was gone.

But the sky was ablaze with the sun, the forest astir with the birds' deafening chatter, and we, the woods—the wooden boles and boughs, the green leaves, the hidden roots—alive with smoothly travelling sap. The days had got longer and had finally overtaken the nights. Light was now brightly set free, unrestrained between the sky, the leaf canopy and me, the last one to receive any direct sunlight, and yet content with the low-intensity halo which reached my leaflets. It was enough for me, and so was the warmth, the kissing of morning dews, and the short-lived starry nights. I recall being agape in wonder, in awe, moonstruck by the enchantment of it all.

I had seen creatures in distress, but no harm had come to me. And, among my many brothers and sisters, I was the only one who had had the privilege of sprouting in mother's immediate proximity. Therefore, only I could directly behold her. How long and lovingly did I gaze at her, through nights and days of spontaneous devotion, I would not know. I do know it was all reciprocated. And life, apart from delightful, seemed to be amusing too.

The bird caught the trout's tail in his beak
and flung her into the lake with a snappy twist of his neck.

For example, the rain was precious. Never in demand, it offered itself abundantly, splashing and spluttering everywhere. It seemed to play with us trees and animals, or even streams and rivers. The latter now and then would protest, and thunder: "Enough!"

Occasionally, the lake overflowed, to the exasperation of some of my lakeside friends, particularly the little ones. All this water was a threat to their safety. Usually, a spirited discussion followed between the sun and the clouds. The former would eventually have his way, if temporarily, and be allowed to cast warm rays which dried us up and made the lake's waters recede. I now realise that those incidents must have not been fun for the lakeside trees, but it all seemed to be a game, not a struggle.

Then I remember noticing that all animals—birds, fish, and mammals alike—ate "things" through their mouths. Later, they discarded something else through an outlet which, regardless of the species, was invariably placed at quite a distance from the mouth. Some of them were phenomenally secretive about this discharging business, while others did it nonchalantly. And, beside that, four-legged animals leaked profusely, though not for long, from either another organ or from apparently the same one. That varied, and I could not account for it. I was personally aware of this because a fox who must have taken a fancy to me bestowed such a liquid all over my leaves. Every day.

What struck me as curious was that what the animals ate voraciously and made quite a fuss about, I had no inclination or use for. However, what they regularly discarded, as if useless and even repugnant, I found rich in elements and put to use.

Weren't we different? They flew, swam, and ran about in earnest; we all stayed put, peacefully. They ate, drank, and then voided; we harvested the elements. Mother, perceiving my curiosity, could not help smiling for, in my seemingly passive way, I must have been an overeager little tree.

Then, one day, a monster appeared. An enormous, four-legged creature with pointy, leafless branches growing out of its head. How could I know that they were the mighty antlers of the red deer? All I knew then was that he and two meeker-looking calves, no pointy branches on their heads, had turned up from nowhere, and were now grazing on bushes, saplings, seedlings. Indeed, on everything green at their mouths' reach. My top was no higher than the smallest calf. I was terror-stricken.

I had nothing against the deer, and they probably were not personally interested in me either, but in my leaves. As they chewed here and there, into their stomachs went the young birches whose fast growth and shiny leaves I had envied. And there went the little alders too. Good grief, the deer were ravenous! Then I saw them come my way.

To my great astonishment, the stag, who I thought was a champion leaf-devourer, pulled his calves beside him and said: "Never, never even lick the yew's leaves. Of all green things in the woods, this is the one you must leave alone."

Off they went, to nibble at something else.

I thought I had had a narrow escape, and was not sure whether the two little ones might eventually disobey their father and return to chew me up. But mother reassured me: "Don't fear, darling. You are in no danger. No harm will come to you from four-legged animals. They nibble at nearly anything, especially in winter, when there's little or no grass and most trees have shed their leaves. Sometimes they are so starved that they eat even the spiny leaves of the young holly trees, at risk of puncturing their gut and dying because of that. But they know better than to eat *our* leaves."

"And why is that, mother?"

"Our leaves are poisonous to them, and so is our bark. Most animals know it, and when the calves are not warned and eat our leaves, they die before long. Our leaves are so bitter that the taste alone should discourage the inexperienced ones, but I suppose that if they lack experience in most things, that includes taste too."

This was good news. I could begin to grasp what the Knowing Cricket had meant when he had lectured me.

No sooner named, no sooner appeared, the go-between turned up, and addressed me with his rasping voice: "Didn't I tell you?

Can't you see that nature craves nothing but this—that the body may be free from distress, and the mind at peace?" Away he leapt, in a hurry.

My nature, as I had just realised, did want just that. But it seemed as if Mother Nature had designed a not quite so peace-loving world. Take, for example, the commonest bird in the forest, the blue tit. Shortly before the longest day in the year, the blue tits' nests would be crowded by nine or ten very hungry fledglings, and their calls could be heard from afar. Their parents had to bring them a caterpillar every minute. Moreover, an adult blue tit fed on one hundred and fifty caterpillars a day. And the ever-threatening sparrow hawk did not need to look far afield for his meals.

An ancient, mighty oak tree had collapsed to the ground after a fierce windstorm. It just lay there, lifeless. I asked: "Do we also fall like that, mother?"

"No. Well, not really. It may happen, but it would take a long, long time. And then again, we may still sprout back."

This was reassuring. I knew it was no lie for we trees cannot say one thing and think differently. So we cannot lie, and we always tell the white and shining truth. Mother added: "My daughter, you are so curious that I'd better tell you something you should know. You see, there exists a natural ranking, and we yews happen to be the high and mighty. You must have noticed already, small as you are, that no harm has come to you from the elements or from the creatures of the air, the earth, the water. Long, very long ago, we were made in order to outlive all creatures, and reign over them."

Having witnessed the end of many seedlings of other species, I had an inkling of something of the sort. These seedlings had been eaten by animals; or shaded out by grown trees, higher and denser; or snatched away by overwhelmingly pelting rain. Now my optimistic hunch was being confirmed by mother.

So far, I had been enjoying myself thoroughly, made some friends, stared at many a sunset, and dreamed as soon as the Evening Star appeared in our northern sky. Now I was learning that there existed a pre-established ranking and that we were at its top. It wasn't a matter of power or prestige. I didn't even know that such things existed. I was just happy for mother and myself, my brothers, sisters, and all kindred souls.

Mother described the hierarchy of the woods.

"Ranking highest, my little darling, is the Yew. The yew is the only living organism which has entirely understood the nature of things; the only being acquainted with all the secrets worth knowing. Also, it is the most long-lived tree in the Land, and the wisest too.

"Below us are all the noble evergreen trees. I want them to be there, it goes without saying, for being evergreen is not only a characteristic, but a state of mind. It means love of life, at all times, in all conditions, even in the dead of winter. Never shed your leaves all at once, keep them green, keep them ready, even if numbed by the cold, for the very first warm sun rays of the season. Be the first one to enjoy them when the higher branches of higher trees are still out of leaf, and let them come through to you.

"There is a cheerful, berried friend, the Holly tree. We hold it in the highest esteem. And there grows the Strawberry Tree, there, by the lake, the jolliest of our sun-loving friends. It can be in bloom and in fruit at the same time; it is always in leaf; and is generous with the birds who love to eat its berries.

"They would both be as fit as we are for leadership, were it not for the fact that they aren't quite as long-lived. Kings and queens have to endure, for the sake of stability and the overall fitness of things.

"Then comes the humble Juniper, somewhat unremarkable, yet berried and generous, resilient, unobtrusive, and faithful to us. Look at that one, over there: its roots never dared come close to mine, though they could have. But it knows better, and we are, after all, distant relatives.

"The stately Pine is very dear to me, what a magnificent being it is! Another well-behaved distant relative, it pays respects and inspires us all with its stature.

"As for the sticky Ivy, well, it's still an evergreen, and I wouldn't blame it just because it isn't strong enough to support itself. It won't harm us, though it may pester other trees, but never strangle them. However, thanks to its flowers and fruits, it attracts insects, that is, food for the birds. And I love birds. So, consider the ivy a privileged vassal of the nobler evergreens. I should add to that category the Heather, but you won't see any of its lovely flowers here, in the shade of the forest.

"Next, I place more berried shrubs, though not evergreen, like Cherries, Crab Apples, Hawthorns and Rowans, all contributing to the well-being of the woods.

"Among the leaf-shedding trees there are two giants: the mighty Oak and the daring Ash. They are powerful and ambitious, though they don't live nearly as long as we do. This explains the oak's willingness to spread its limbs in all directions, and the ash's eagerness to break through the canopy and rise towards the sky. Though we've had some skirmishes over the millennia, they're under control now. By shedding millions of leaves every autumn, they enrich the soil and thus enrich us all.

"I should also mention the handsome Elm. However, it has been cleared away to such an extent that I doubt whether it will survive in the future."

"Cleared away," mother had said. I ought to have asked: "by what?" But I was too taken by her words, did not interrupt her, and soon forgot.

"Next is the Hazel, which is magic and feeds many a living thing—once, even the Salmon of Knowledge fed on its nuts.

"Birch, Alder and Willow all grow fast and all die fast; all love water and all to water succumb when prolonged floods choke them. They're lovely, but dim-witted, and still have much to learn. So, never emulate them.

"All the lower plants are just that, of course, but not to be ignored or frowned upon. All flowers, herbs, ferns, mosses, lichens and so on are part of the Garden of Earthly Delights, and our Land would not be the same without them.

"New species may come to our shores in the future, one way or the other. No matter how impressive they may be, never be dazzled, for the Yew is king and queen, and, by then, *yew* shall be the queen."

Quite a burden for a seedling who had just got over the horror of nearly being chewed up by two inexperienced calves, but I didn't really care. Perhaps my fuzzy memory had been able to let only that piece of intelligence get through to me: that I was born a... what? A princess, it appeared. And that therefore there was precious little to worry about.

Growing was an unconscious effort. Indeed, it all seemed quite effortless. I was aware that I was growing unhurriedly, day by day, night by night. But, should you have asked, I wouldn't have had the faintest clue as to how the magic occurred. For magic it must be.

In these early years, I remember hardly any direct sunlight, much rain, and not a little wind. Everything was just fine. A baby of yours would not be aware of her breathing; she would not know, as I did not know, what was involved. But, unlike a baby, I suspected, I felt, that everything was all right.

One breezy day in early spring, my third spring, I saw some puffy clouds glide along. They were low, very low clouds, and not damp and cold. It was a lovely day, and the puffy clouds kept fluttering about. Puzzled, I asked: "Mother, what kind of clouds are those?"

"Those are not clouds, my darling. That's love, a most ethereal thing."

"I love you too, mother. But I don't make anything like that."

"Of course not. This type of love is called pollen."

"Pollen?"

"Yes, my little one. This cloud comes from your father."

My father! What else could I ask for? I had the Garden of Earthly Delights all for me, and my mother telling me such wonderful things.

I remember singing to myself, sometimes. I was no melodious bird, nor did I have my way with words like the Knowing Cricket. My song for mother was simple, and sincere.

> She's all that I need
> She's all that I want
> And that's all...

And again, over and over again:

> She's all that I need
> She's all that I want
> And that's all...

But that was *not* all.

THREE

When I first found out about them I must have been twenty or thirty springs old. It all happened one night. I remember some dim, silvery light from a crescent moon, shortly after sundown, at the beginning of summer.

I was a strong, promising (and rather attractive) sapling, as tall as my nature would allow, and that is, as high as the red stag's mighty antlers. From there I could see farther afield. But I was not the first one, that night, to hear strange noises, somewhere in the distance. The whole forest suddenly grew silent. Leaves atremble, all animals afraid, the woods echoed with fear. Never had I seen wolves, stags and even bears run away in a stampede from what must have been imminent danger. It reached me so quickly that I did not have time to inquire about it with mother.

They were already near us, by us. Four extraordinarily outlandish animals, never seen before. Unlike plants, they were made up of a system of loosely connected parts, yet all very symmetrical, as in all inferior beings. However, unlike the animals I knew, they were two-legged, yet had no wings, but two paws. These they used to brandish things I also had never seen before—weapons, as I was to learn, and other oddly shaped objects. Despite their upright posture, they were sure-footed and fairly agile. One of these beasts was stark-naked, I thought, for nothing queer hung from his body. Two of them were covered with skins which once must have belonged to other animals. The tallest one was white-garbed, with the colour of the blood—as I had seen it seep from wolves' prey—in his cheeks; the colour of the snow in his hairless skin; and the colour of the hot sun in his hair.

I could feel, almost smell, the coming of something dreadful, something similar to what I sensed when the sparrow hawk closed in on its prey and but a breath of life was left in it. But the frenzy of the chase was not there. No desperate flying or running about. The naked beast had been obviously overpowered, yet the killing of the prey had been postponed. Why? I had seldom seen kindred animals fight one other, and when it did happen, it was quick, just like the flash of death. But this, this was something else.

The white-garbed beast addressed a few mutters to the waning moon. Then he spoke to the skin-covered beasts, who in turn shouted something at the naked one. Louder and louder words were exchanged—I presumed they were words although I could not understand them—and something began to happen.

It was as if flames leapt from the beasts' flashing eyes. Then a fire of unrestrained wrath broke out, and the three clothed beasts blazed to sudden rage. I felt such terrible heat mount amid their shrieks that I thought their own fury might burst them apart from within. One of the skin-covered beasts took hold of a sword and slashed the naked one beneath his head. The wounded beast collapsed.

"Supper at last," I thought, assuming that these animals fed on one another. However, the three stood back, and the white-garbed one observed the frantic spasms of the mortally wounded wretch, and the flowing of his blood as it streamed out of the wound, as if attempting to divine something.

This performance was supremely odd. What exceptionally deviant beasts these must be! They had reached our grove deliberately, with their victim-to-be. Then they had staged an apparently rehearsed slaying, preceded by invocations, inspired by a sudden rise in their body temperature, yet followed by cold-blooded observations. When death had come, they had left, as suddenly as they had arrived, making no further use of their prey. No other animal I knew behaved this way.

The reawakening of the woods was as magical as ever, with leaves aflutter in the morning breezes, and Mother Nature's dew-dabbed kisses. But other thoughts engaged me, and somehow spoilt the enchantment. Whom could I ask about the outlandish creatures of the day before, and their strange behaviour?

As I was about to ask mother, a wolf pack stealthily came my way. I supposed they might satisfy my curiosity, for I had seen them, once, gorge on a deer and reduce his carcass to hair and bones. I thought they might know about those other beasts; perhaps, even understand them. I ventured: "Would you mind answering some questions?"

"If we must," replied the leader, an old and scruffy wolf who looked as if he could not be bothered, yet he would, for no-one in the forest dared not to respect us yews.

"Would you happen to know something about some odd, two-legged creatures, who keep their heads high, use their paws to hold odd things, and kill their prey with elaborate preambles, yet they do not eat it?"

"It is man that you probably mean."

"Man?"

"Yes, man."

"I see. And what about this... man creature?"

"What about him?"

"Listen, you rude quadruped: you said you would tell me about this 'man'. Surely, you don't mean to put me off with your curt replies?"

"If I may," a conciliatory voice intervened, "I think I could answer your questions."

"And who would you be?"

A most remarkable she-wolf, as it transpired. She descended from that highborn she-wolf who, centuries before, had suckled two twin baby boys who were to found a great city and, in turn, a great civilisation. But history's wayward unfolding had made her family wander to this distant Land, where she had lived all her life, albeit not forgetful of her lineage. Therefore, she suggested that we could have a conversation "as equals."

"I, a quadruped's equal?" I thought, aghast. Pretending not to hear this absurdity, I encouraged her to speak.

...observed the frantic spasms of the mortally wounded wretch, and the flowing of his blood as it streamed out of the wound.

"You see, man is somewhat like us wolves. They too mate for life."

"Really? How peculiar. And why is that?"

"We and they claim it's got to do with love, but I think it's more a matter of convenience. It makes for a more manageable society. They also have leaders, and a social structure. But here's where the similarities end. I've been told that a long, long time ago, they stopped crawling on all fours and attained their odd upright posture. Soon they started wondering what they could do with their paws, which they call arms. And, legend has it, they began to use them, their arms and hands, to make things, objects for different purposes. Since then, they've spent much time in figuring out what to invent next; how to put it to use; how to prevent another tribe getting hold of it; and how to go to war with this other tribe."

"I *have* noticed their keenness on warlike pursuits."

"Oh, you haven't seen anything yet! We too like to stalk, and chase, and kill, but men have outdone us, they've taken it all a step farther. We hunt after our food. We may enjoy doing so, but at the same time we *have* to do so. They hunt after their food *and* their pleasure."

"Pleasure? What do you mean by that?"

"Let her find out for herself," the pack leader jumped in, and added: "listen, lady Little Tree," (imagine that! Only a boor would not address me by my title), "we are off again to the next chase, but we'll see each other soon, I'm sure."

Off they went.

"And women are no different," whispered a gentle voice coming from somewhere below. It belonged to a butterwort, a pretty violet flower which grew between two birches, in a wettish site not far from me.

"Women are just like men?" I asked, puzzled.

"They're gentler, and not quite as untidy. But whenever they spot one of us pretty flowers, all too many of them pluck us so that they may bedeck their hair or dwellings. I mean, really, what vanity!"

She might have been convincing had I not seen her and many more butterworts engage in a rather distasteful activity. They would secrete a fluid as their leaves rolled up at the edges so as to trap and digest insects. That made not only for a sticky plant,

but also for a distinctively *not* plantlike behaviour. So I paid little
or no attention to her complaint.

But soon word reached me from two kindlier flowers, the rosy-
purple bitter vetch and the yellow and red bird's foot trefoil. They
both said that, indeed, women plucked flowers left and right.
Because of that, most if not all flowers disliked them and feared
them more than men, who left them undisturbed.

From the darker woods, the woolly mosses added, discreetly
but firmly: "Men and women alike won't think twice about
stepping over us. Sometimes they need to cross the woods with
their cattle and horses. They trample over us carelessly, leaving a
battlefield where a smooth green carpet used to be."

A brownish snake slithered along and revealed: "They think
the worst of us snakes, though we don't prey on their livestock
and don't bother them in any way. In fact, they hardly ever see us.
But when they do spot us, they immediately strike us, and often
succeed at chopping our heads off."

I thought man must have a morbid fascination with heads. I
had seen them slash one of their victim's throat; then the snake
had told me about their cleaving habit; and a few days later I
caught a glimpse of a few warriors galloping on horseback in the
distance. To my shock and horror, I noticed a few human heads
hanging by the horses' manes. Head-hunters! Since I knew that
animals' thinking organs resided in their head, I realised that
there was no better way to impair a body than by beheading it.
Indeed, once the head was detached from the body, death ensued.

I assumed that man had invented swords and other blades so
that he could systematically behead all kinds of creatures. It was
then that a towering elm tree said: "I wish they had limited their
cutting obsession to fellow animals. But they'll stop at nothing.
They've also invented other instruments of death, like axes.
Those concern us. You see, not all of them call us trees. For some
we are 'timber'. Our boles and boughs become posts, planks and
logs for the construction of their homes, boats and even roads.
Ironically, their axes, mattocks, picks and adzes are all fitted with
wooden handles. That has given them tremendous leverage.
There's little difference between stone and metal axes. The
wooden handle has made the difference.

"We elms used to thrive by the tens of thousands. But man came into the Land, spread like a blight, and began to clear the woods. Since brush required grubbing and cutting and much work, they understood that the larger the trees, the better. So they turned their energies to thousands of us mighty trees. First, they'd girdle us, ring-bark us. Then, they'd let us die. Finally, they'd clear the forest litter by burning. Man has learned to do that too, to summon fire whenever he needs it. You can't imagine how many hazels, ashes, hawthorns and hollies have been burned by man.

"Look at me now, and behold me, for our clearing has been so merciless, I don't know if we have any future in this Land."

Good grief! What was wrong with this man-creature? Suddenly, it felt as though I could hear a choral crooning coming from all the beings in the forest:

> Man is wicked
> wicked, wicked;
> man is wicked
> very wicked.

The same wolf pack soon returned to our grove. The scruffy leader, who appeared to be in a slightly better disposition, bid me a good morning and said: "It's been a memorable night, you should have been there. You must know by now that man has built many ring forts to defend his people from other tribes, and his livestock from us. Yesterday we discovered a passage leading into the fort, and oddly enough the fort had no man in it, but with all his livestock. We slaughtered them all. It was too good to be true, all those fat cattle and sheep at the mercy of our fangs."

"I wonder why they weren't there?" the she-wolf commented, and went on to say: "if only you knew how many traps they can come up with, you'd understand why we couldn't believe our luck."

That was enough savagery for a young princess, and I turned to my mother in despair, hoping that she could deny the things I had heard. She said: "Do you wish to know why the men and

women and children have apparently abandoned their fort, my
darling? Look over there."

There came a group of fair-skinned people, with reddish or
fair long hair, blue eyes, and clothed with strange cloaks made of
other animals' skins or some peculiar material I had never seen.
One of them, with a deep-sounding and very harsh voice, ordered
them about. I took him to be the king. He was immediately
followed by the white-garbed man by the long beard. Then came
what my mother told me was their whole tribe, with women and
men, and miniature men and women which were, in fact,
children. They all stopped near my mother. The white-garbed
man, their druid, uttered invocations and magic formulæ. He
gesticulated in the air above his head, directing his words to the
sky, and then said: "All is done. This is our new sacred grove, over
which the yew is sovereign."

The crowd quickly dispersed and probably went back to the
fort, where the wolves' surprise awaited them. All things
considered, this was the first good news in quite a while.

"Of course, my dear," my mother whispered, "it is not all that
bad. These people, no matter how crude they are, believe that
there is an earth-mother from whom we spring and to whom we
return. They believe that the Spirit inhabits rocks, heights,
mountains; that the Spirit illuminates rivers and streams and
the darkness of lakes. And most crucially, they have understood
that the Spirit belongs to trees, particularly to us yew trees. We
are the medium between their world and the Otherworld. They'll
pray by us; we'll be their tribe's rallying-point; they'll invoke their
gods by the water we drink from. A few summers ago I told you:
Yew shall be queen. It was a prophecy, and this is its fulfilment.
You have nothing to fear from these men, my darling. On the
contrary, not only shall they respect us, but they shall venerate
us."

I felt relieved and very happy, also for the few elms that lived
in our woods, for I knew that at least here no harm would come
to them. Had I been slightly more discerning, I would have
wondered why my mother had said that we had nothing to fear
from *these* men, rather than nothing to fear from man in general.
I suppose I was still too young, and too enthralled with the idea

of having been consecrated as the princess and future queen of the forest.

Besides, how could man be such a monster, after all? In the turmoil of those momentous days, I had forgotten the slain man. But, as I looked for him, I could not see his corpse anywhere.

I know now that the woods' waste-disposal team had been at work all along. A staggering number of bacteria, weevils, beetles, worms, bugs of all types, even birds and, last but not least, some prodigiously voracious badgers, had devoured the wretched man's flesh. But for a few scattered bones, the ill-fated earthling had gone back to the Earth, as all animals seemed to do. And the few bones that were left did not look all that almighty. They reassured me about the fact that man was no exception. As all other animals, he too appeared to be merely transient.

FOUR

I was awakening to my 122nd spring, and the rain was there, as ever, to greet me. It used to rain, and still does, every other day, sometimes even every day, and when it did not rain, it rained harder. I had noticed that man was not keen on this constant downpour. Therefore, although the local tribe had elected our woods as its sacred grove, I did not see much of its members. I, on the contrary, loved the rain, and so did most of the other plants.

I remember waking that year under a veritable deluge, and saying to my mother, who was still dormant and seemed not ready to reawaken: "Mother, mother, wake up! Spring is sprung."

"Oh yes, spring, my little one. That's right," she answered at length, drowsily.

How could she not be as happy as I was? We yews were always the first ones to come out of our wintry slumber and to rejoice as the first glimmers of the northern spring appeared. I realise now that perhaps the miracle of life anew after the dead of winter may not be that enticing when it happens for the umpteenth time. Perhaps it felt more like a habit than a miracle. Possibly my mother, having reached a venerable age, would have rather slept on. Not I, though, not at all. In autumn, I was always the last one to go to sleep, reluctantly. And, in spring, the first one to wake.

Life was lovely, and... so was I. By now I had reached a respectable size. My bole was slender; my bark, beige and purplish where not covered by green, smooth mosses. My boughs were graceful, yet strong. My foliage, thick and luxuriant, was dark green when seen from the sky and, beneath, of a pale lemon colour. For a few seasons I had been coming into fruit, at first bashfully, as all young women. According to the chirpy birds, my berries were the sweetest ones. According to my suitors—many a handsome yew in the forest and yonder—their red was the brightest colour in the shade of the woods.

As my mother had predicted, my coeval birches, alders and willows had by then come and gone. Their offspring were now keeping us company, and I knew that I would outlive them too. The almost bare limestone upon which I grew would have sustained little if any life, but I had my roots artfully burrow into it, and develop over it, underground and aboveground. Unlike all other trees, I could make myself at home anywhere. And I loved my home, and the skies above it.

During cloudless nights, on the blue depth the stars sparkled, greenish, yellow, white, rose, brighter, flashing more like gems and jewels. In those enchanting nights I often marvelled if I could, not knowing how, hear the resonances of countless kindred souls?

I had learned a great deal, about man too, starting with his language. (In retrospect, I realise that once I had learned the specific language spoken by the tribe which worshipped me, I had learned all man's languages. They all sounded different, but all came from the same source, and I have heard and understood many different human tongues since those days.) From my friends, the migratory birds, I had learned the layout of lands and seas over the Earth.

What I had hitherto called the "Land" was in fact a land encircled by the waters of the salt-sea oceans. In other words, an Island. And next to my leafy Island, across a stretch of sea in the direction of the rising sun, lay another island, larger by far.

Before my birth, many tribes from a vast Land, a Continent, had come over to this larger island, and settled in it. Then, a different type of man had come from sunnier lands of the Continent. He had come to conquer and to occupy. A warlike man led these newcomers. Their military and organisational skills were so formidable that they quickly triumphed over the natives. After repeated wars, these soldierly people, the Romans, set about the pacification and the defence of the island they had partially invaded, giving rise to a complex society.

Their troops, fifty-five thousands of them, were the heart of the colonial society. The army was made up of legions, which were divided into cohorts and in turn subdivided into centuries. Each legion was commanded by a prætor who had reached the rank of senator. His staff consisted of six military tribunes, though in battle the effective leadership was entrusted to the centurions. It was a complex, though smoothly-running, war machine. Nothing like it had come to that island before.

In the spring of my 122nd reawakening, one of the six tribunes in command of the IX Hispana Legion, then in charge of the island, devised an ambitious plan. Rumour had reached his ears that, somewhere back in the centre of the Empire, the emperor had decided personally to embark on the long voyage to the island. He would be leading along a new legion which was to replace the IX Hispana. Professedly, he intended to build a stupendous wall to use as a border. It was also said that he intended to survey the neighbouring island Hibernia, my Island, and see if conquering it might be worthwhile.

"If I took care of that," the tribune thought, "and delivered a conquered Hibernia to the emperor on a silver tray, I'd be rewarded with the rank of prætor. And soon enough of senator."

The tribune was an utterly self-made man. Of peasant stock, he had felt drawn to the military life when still a boy. In a time of colonial expansion, such men were cherished by the military machine. Within a few years, owing to his skilful handling of the sword and his ruthless tactics in the battlefield, he had gained the reputation of a warlord. As such, he had been dispatched to the island, where he had outdone himself. When it came to suppressing uprisings, he invariably drowned them in bloodbaths.

Between military campaigns, he had also wedded a resilient woman who had borne him a baby boy before her resilience gave way and she committed adultery with a native. This situation resulted in having both lovers killed and the son raised by a nurse, then a nanny, and eventually by the army.

His son Aeneas, a shy and sickly chap, entered the army at the age of twelve. His father provided no particular protection for him. He believed in rising from the ranks and was confident that his son would not disappoint him.

It was a take-it-or-leave-it arrangement, though leave he could not. He managed to stay alive, and eventually became skilful in the use of the double-bladed sword, the dagger and the javelin. He also grew accustomed to marching, swimming and stone-slinging; as well as horseback riding, including being able to mount and dismount fully armed with shield and equipment. Beside these strictly military skills, he was also expected to dig and to build a camp, which involved handling and moving earth, turf, timber and stone. Finally, he also had to work in road-building, quarrying and canal-digging.

The father, whose minions monitored Aeneas, made sure that he would keep to his duties like any ordinary soldier. Such duties had meant, from time to time, actual fighting, fear and its natural antidote—bravery. Fighting, he had soon realised, meant either to kill or to be killed. Though he encountered great difficulty in bringing himself to hate an unknown, impersonal enemy, hate he must, for he was not able to kill cold-bloodedly. He did not particularly like hunting, and was probably one of the few Roman soldiers who enjoyed his daily ration of porridge and vegetables, preferring them over meat.

In time, he rose to the rank of chief centurion. He had had enough of back-breaking jobs under cold, pelting rain. It was then that his father conceived his plan. He would send his son over to Hibernia as the leader of a good part of the legion; and have him conquer the Island on his behalf, so as to present it to the emperor as a personal gift from his loyal military tribune.

The navy hastily readied a large fleet of galleys to ferry the troops across the channel between the two islands.

As soon as the soldiers set foot on the Island, I could perceive their heavy tread upon our soil. Trees in a forest are all interconnected by the filaments of an underground network of fungi. Consequently, what I am about to tell you is no longer hearsay, but direct knowledge of the events.

Within a few days, Aeneas persuaded his troops that the Island was inhabited by the most viciously warlike people one could imagine.

"If life is dear to you and to your loved ones," he said, "I order you to build a stone fort. It will protect us from the raids of these warriors. Once you'll be done with the construction of the fort, you shall seek shelter within it, and stay put until I return. Do as I say."

The question on every soldier's mind was: "Return? From where?"

Aeneas told the troops that he would wander, in disguise, so as to survey the Island and verify whether or not it was worth a war.

"No-one must know of this plot, back in Britannia," he warned, "lest it be jeopardised."

Accompanied by his most faithful friend, rid of their corslets and kilts, but rather clothed as the natives, the two of them left on horseback on an early spring day.

As they wandered, seemingly aimlessly, further in and further up, roaming all over the Island; as they met with people and befriended them; as they savoured the softness of the drizzle, the twinkling of a starry sky, and the freedom afforded by a wholly unregimented life, it became apparent that Aeneas was the errant son of an unerring father. Never had he felt so alive. No hard work to be done. Some fishing and occasional hunting—joined with the generosity of the natives they met now and then—took care of their hunger. A tent for shelter, water and grass for the horses to be had anywhere. And under the vast, overwhelming skies, home was in them wherever they roamed.

Aeneas began to think about the duties and the authoritarian father he had left behind, but then put his face to the wind and said to his friend: "The wind is delicious. It's carrying the scent of a thousand flowers. Let's follow it to its birthplace."

One of my best friends, a strawberry tree which grew by the lake shore, saw them first. They were walking, holding their horses by the reins, chatting. As they spent many words in praise of the woods, I took an instant liking to them, especially to Aeneas. He was not as tall as the tribesmen I was used to, nor was his skin as fair. And his hair was short and of the same brown as the hazel's. He spoke a carefully structured language, which, in his mouth, sounded oddly over-organised, just as his life had been, or that of any soldier.

They knotted the horses' reins round my bole. I found it flattering that a man who had come from so far away, the head of a dreadfully powerful legion, would pick me, without hesitation, as his first choice. And not only for his horse, but also as a camping site. Though it was still broad daylight, he already told his friend to pitch the tent and prepare for a long sleep.

Sleeping was what he had been deprived of all his life and what he liked the most among the things he had experienced since leaving the troops. As you can imagine, I quite disagreed, and felt inspired to voice my dissent by dropping some dried-up twigs. But then I decided to let things go their way. The sun was just beginning to set then, yet the men were already inside the tent, under their covers, Aeneas fast asleep.

As they lay wrapped in their sleeping furs, the lake's water foamed briefly, night fell, and a shape slid gracefully out of the waves. The Fairy Maid of the Lake rose and stepped onto the little beach, close to the strawberry tree, fully in my sight. She had a mane of long and winding black hair glittering with emerald highlights. Her only garment, a cloak, she unclasped, and laid down on the sand.

I had never seen her, or anything like her, before. However, I was not startled. Although her apparition was doubtless uncanny, she was as shapely as the nature of human women would allow, her body a curvaceous fusion of gentle bends which told of an overall appealing roundness.

She might have been a vision—but she was real. She began to sing, loudly enough to awaken the men. Presently, the soldier came out of the tent, squeezed his eyes towards the lake, then rubbed them, then squeezed them again, astonished.

"Centurion, Centurion!" he cried, plunging back into the small tent. "By the lake shore, on the beach: there's a naked woman, or a fairy, I don't know."

"Is she cold?"

"What do you mean, *is she cold?*"

"Just that."

"Well, I suppose not, I mean, there's a mantle of sorts by her feet. If she were cold, she'd wear it."

"Then, let her be and, please, let me sleep."

"But, my lord, this reeks of sorcery."

"Then let it reek, and let me sleep."

"But, my lord, what if she sent forth smoke and stench?"

"Is she?"

"No, not for the moment, but…"

"You roused me from sleep. There's no going back for a while now, so let me have a look." Out of the tent came the young man. "Who are you?" he asked.

She answered in his tongue: "I am that which you crave." As she spoke, her eyes snapped open, emerald green in the pale moonlight. She went on: "Though you've taken the life of many men, you're yet to know woman."

"That's true," Aeneas admitted to himself, though he wished she had not acquainted his soldier with his sentimental life. "Which," he thought, "I've never had. Never had a woman, love, or even a moment of total, unconditional surrender." He said: "Soldier, go fetch me a pheasant."

"Now? At this time in the night?"

"Yes, now. And if you don't find any, look for it all night."

As the disgruntled soldier moved his steps towards God knows what pheasant (which did *not* exist on the Island as of yet), Aeneas, stripped of any fear, walked to the beach.

"Here comes my prey," the Fairy Maid thought. "I shall take him to the bottom of the lake, and leave him there forever."

The stars were bright, and magic was afoot. Aeneas knelt before her and said: "Oh creature of the waters, oh Fairy Maid, if that is what thou art… I am the leader of a great army, an army this Island could not repel. Thou can sink me to the dark bottom of the lake, and what care I if I should die? Or what care I if I should be forever bound to the depths of a bottomless lake? I was bound all my life, and forced to do things… atrocious, in whose name and for whose sake I no longer know. But if I should vanish, my soldier would come to know. Then he would return to the fort and tell the troops. They would seek me, and destroy and kill everything and everybody in their way."

Suddenly, he took her in his arms and kissed her.

I remember asking to myself: "Is that pleasure, I wonder?" And, who should turn up but the Knowing Cricket? He had been missing for quite a while, fifty summers, more or less.

"Yes, my lady yew, that is pleasure," he whispered. He told me that he had been planet-hopping for a few of "our" years, and I didn't believe him. But I did believe him when he added: "I know this Fairy Maid. She used to dwell in the great salt-sea ocean. She's changed waters, I take it, but not habits, I'm afraid."

As we looked at them, and as we saw their dreams and lives become entwined, we felt that something extraordinary was about to happen.

"I've never seen it like this," the Knowing Cricket continued. "There's no deceit, here. We may be in for a surprise."

At the same time, miles and miles away, thousands of graceful fairies beguiled the troops out and away from the fort. The following days, weeks, and months, they accompanied them throughout the Island; had them befriend the people; and find themselves brides. In time, they all forgot the Empire, and the invasion of this Island.

Back in Britannia, the emperor took them for slain by the ferocious native fighters; replaced them with a new legion, the VI Victrix; and forgot the Island altogether, busy as he was with the construction of a wall which was to bear his name—Hadrian.

Aeneas's father was sent back to Rome, there to be put on trial for high treason and abuse of power. Unanimously found guilty, he was sentenced to death, and thereon executed. Indeed, his conduct was deemed so shameful and un-Roman that his trial's records were burned in an attempt to obliterate him from history.

This is how the IX Hispana Legion "vanished" from the annals of history and from the face of the Earth.

This also explains why the Romans never did invade and conquer my Island.

As for Aeneas, this is what happened.

Thousands of graceful fairies beguiled the troops out and away from the fort.

For the first time in her long life, the Fairy Maid felt that she had been loved, rather than treated as an appeaser of the senses. The young man, who had never loved before, wanted to know no other love, and cared little for the battles of this world. By not sinking him to the bottom of the lake, the Maid knew what would become of her, and of him, since there was no disjoining them anymore. They would ascend to the Land of the Ever Placid, a place too calm for most human beings. But Aeneas had discovered he was positively keen on sleeping, while the Maid had had enough of deceiving men.

Up to the Land of the Ever Placid they flew, never to be seen by mortal eyes again.

FIVE

Not far from where I lived, away from the lake, towards the rising sun, there was an oak which was a mere sapling at the time of Aeneas and the Fairy Maid. By now, however, it had grown into a majestic matriarch. I will not sing the oak's praises for it must not be forgotten that, among the non-evergreen trees, it stood the closest to us yews, just a step below in the tree hierarchy. No monarch should in any way encourage a potential usurper. Suffice it to say that, in its 340-odd years of fruitful life, it had produced about eighteen million acorns. I could do away with "odd" and "about" and tell the exact number of years it had been in existence and the exact number of offspring it had generated, were I not somewhat embarrassed by that. I mean, you may wonder about my sanity.

Yet, not only did I keep account of all the acorns I had observed down the centuries sitting tight to its twigs, but I even kept track of the ever-changing routes that slugs, ants, spiders, beetles, weevils and caterpillars followed up and down its trunk. Why, I had innumerable hours to while away, more than a human could possibly appreciate.

Once I understood that the artistry in a yew's life lay in casting off all ingredients inimical to well-being; once I realised that I was naturally predestined to keep away from trouble, I concluded against my mother's advice that concentrating solely on the elimination of non-essentials was simply no fun. I merely had to grow, unhurriedly, and invent pastimes. How could I tell what was essential and inessential? So I counted the acorns, tracked the bugs, and watched the stars and their position in relation to the changing of the seasons.

The most engaging amusement to be had, man and his activities, had been in short supply for a good three centuries.

Druidical ceremonies were held in our grove from time to time, and at first I used to find them intriguing. But I eventually tired of them, for they were kept perfectly unaltered. From a human standpoint, this might have been a virtue, but it made for a repetitive show and turned the extraordinary into the ordinary. Sometimes, a druid would turn up on his own in the woods, led by—or leading?—his hazel wand. He would cut off some of mother's leafy twigs so as to use them for magical purposes.

As for human sacrifices, only two had been carried out since my fateful introduction to mankind. The Fairy Maid of the Lake had flown up and off irrevocably. Occasional tribesmen hunted deer, or boars, or, for a day's sport, even foxes and hares. Their appearances were rare and they hardly ever caught anything, at least within my sight.

The other trees provided a more continuous show. The strawberry tree by the lake shore was my favourite above all. We were born in the same year and, just like me, it was still standing, as airily as ever. Many times I had seen it collapse under its own weight, or the snow's, or under the pressure of the wind. Yet, just as many times I had seen it sprout back and start anew. Its trunk and branches, therefore, were newly born, but the bulk of its roots was as old as its soul.

This pattern probably accounted for its exuberance: constant rejuvenescence, with aged roots to accompany an aged soul, young branches and twigs to inspire fresh experiences, and a profusion of thanks-giving blooms and fruits.

Then there was "the champion bearer", a towering ash. Although hit seven times by lightning, although scalded and scarred, it had withstood them all, and was still standing, the tallest lightning rod in the forest. Such dauntless determination did not fail to exert a certain charm among other plants. That was why ivy, gradually and affectionately, grew to enwrap it utterly.

The vine bedecked the ash with shiny green leaves climbing round the bole, which, being shaded by the thick leaf canopy, was utterly branchless. Not that it had much in the way of boughs and leaves once it broke through the canopy on its way to the sky— and the lightning—but enough for the chlorophyll in its leaves to absorb energy from the sun.

It was only later in my life that I began to understand that natural, sporadic pruning could be to the advantage of our well-being, by promoting new tissue and new shoots. In the instance of lightning, such a pruning could even promote a new leading shoot, or several new shoots, or a thick head of branches in their stead.

That was how, I conjectured, my mother had come to look the way she did. Windstorms, lightning, heavy snowfall and, naturally, great age, had all contributed to her aspect. Her top had been blown off by a windstorm which had set the whole forest atremble and caused damage to most trees. However, a crop of young shoots, stemming from where the breakage had occurred, had ensued. These new shoots, too many of them, competed for light and air, overcrowded one another, and only a few eventually grew into branches, while the other ones died back.

Her venerable trunk had been hollow for centuries. No cause for alarm, though, for she herself had told me that all yews of great age get rid of their dead wood.

Her crown was most irregular, with many dried twigs and branchlets, and only her higher boughs were not entirely destitute of foliage. Sizeable burls and knots had grown over ancient and recent fissures, the vestiges of innumerable mutilations provoked by storms. As a result, the rule in her features was utmost asymmetry.

Not that we trees value symmetry, for that pertains to inferior beings. But my mother had certainly outdone asymmetry itself, for she looked more like a random aggregation of woody tissue and leaves than like a regular tree. But then again, how could "regular" apply to the Queen of the Forest?

In time I realised that her wondrously shaggy appearance constituted the emblem of true great age and accomplished matriarchy. That, however, was a taste to be acquired. I must confess that I was proud of my powerful trunk, sound to the centre, and of my ever-increasing dark green, pale yellow foliage.

What little colour could be traced on mother was provided by a thin film of green algæ which had covered a good part of her body where the bark had fallen off. Lichens prospered round her gnarled limbs and even within her trunk's vast cavity, and so did mosses. Yet, time and again she had said: "Don't worry, my beautiful one. Someday you'll understand. I've merely slowed down. The less the growth, the less the effort. I'm quite content with my present size and with keeping evergreen. I love you, and all the plants in my forest."

Her love was reciprocated. Some flowers, for example, had sprung up beneath her, forming a thick bed of bluish-mauve gypsy roses, something previously unseen in the deep shade of our woods. But deep shade was something my mother's withered boughs and foliage no longer cast. Between rain showers and downpours, the flowers were constantly visited by bees and butterflies. Even some reticent snakes came to look my mother up, slithering gracefully through the flowers. And the deer had made their new place of congregation round her. With uncharacteristic mindfulness, neither did they graze nor did they tramp on the flowers.

Lately, a curious-looking bird, the treecreeper, had made its presence felt on her limbs. It climbed jerkily up her trunk, or up what had become of it, looking more like a mouse, actually. Yet, it was a pretty little thing, with its back mimetically painted with amber, brown and grey hues. Its longish and stiff tail feathers propped it against the tree where its thin curved bill dragged out the weevils and beetles on which it fed.

There were quite a number of them, nestling behind the flaps of mother's peeling bark. I liked them. With their incessant trailing up and down her body, they kept her company, kept her pest-free and, she told me smilingly, they even gently... tickled her. I never marvelled at there not being any treecreepers on me. I assumed that they might not get on well with the dozens of coal tits and tiny goldcrests which dwelled amid my boughs. Moreover, I was busy, not just counting acorns or star-gazing, but rather because of my involvement in a sort of remote motherhood.

I had been blooming and bearing berries for many years. Sadly, only a few of my offspring had managed to sprout, and then withstand the treacheries of the elements. In spite of that, many a daughter and a son of mine had been born, though not within my sight. Both the wind and birds had dispersed them, or, occasionally, an invariably voracious badger who would gulp down some of my berries. By now, tens and tens of them were growing. I could not see them, but I could at least *feel* them. I did not know how, yet, but in some way other than through underground filaments. My daughters' and sons' signals must come through some sort of field. As for what field, that I could not fathom.

Then there were the reports from fellow trees. The news would originate with one of my offspring, then bounce from tree to tree till it reached me. That is why I had let so many birds live upon me: they were the most direct messengers to and from my daughters and sons. Every day, they flew to every one of them, bringing them my love, and carrying theirs back to me.

One evening just after sundown, a lofty pine whispered something. Everyone in the forest grew silent, for it was anything but a loquacious tree, and his words were as rare as they were significant.

"Look up in the skies," it said, "perhaps as far as fifty miles high. Can you see those clouds? They're shining eerily in the aftermath of the day that's done. This is an omen. Something is about to happen."

The clouds continued to shine long after sunset, (so I was told, the next day, by a fox), tinting the skies with a coloured, yet disturbing, glow. They did not belong there at a time in which light gives way to darkness and stars come alive. There was a peculiar feeling of displacement in the air, but also one of scepticism. My mother paid little if any attention to the purported oracle.

"A very well-meaning tree," she said, "by all means, but... It takes me longer than it takes you, my friends, to go sleep, at night—you know, my enormous root network, all that sap, so much inertia. So, when I eventually trail into sleep, I often see the very same spectacle that puzzles the pine so. It just happens to have come earlier, tonight. Go to sleep, my dear ones. Don't worry."

We were already dozing off, dear mother, and perhaps you were right, as usual. There was probably nothing to worry about, or even to expect.

And so it was. For two or three moons, little if anything happened. Actually, our champion bearer, the ash, was hit by lightning for the eighth time in its life, but, in its own words, it was "a trifling bolt." Then, one rainy morning, odd things came our way.

Our sentinel/lightning rod diverted our attention from the fun of showering after dawn on a summer day.

"Seven men abroad, down yonder!" it screamed, and then corrected itself: "Eight men, white-dressed, walking towards us in the rain, down yonder."

"Are you quite sure?" I asked. "It would be most uncommon, wouldn't it?"

"Why, I reckon it would, but that's exactly what I'm beholding: eight white-dressed men, walking towards the woods. And walking solemnly, not jerkily, as men do when caught in the rain."

"Pardon my saying so, but would it seem entirely inappropriate to say that you are hallucinating?"

"Why would that be?"

"All those thunderbolts may as well have had some repercussions."

"Not at all! I'm the champion bearer, am I not? But you must believe me: there's a whole congregation of men marching headlong into their sacred grove, and that is, us."

"Just listen to my ash, will you? Why shouldn't you believe it?"

The enwrapping (and enamoured) ivy had spoken. I wouldn't have let her get away with addressing me so insolently had not the druids suddenly appeared, by mother's gypsy roses.

Among the seven more simply clothed druids there stood the only one I knew, the same one who occasionally turned up in our grove. All the others were unknown, and must have come from afar. The eighth man was evidently their leader.

His pensive grey eyes told of great authority, great occult powers, but also of profound preoccupation. He was the Island's Arch-Druid. No-one in the religious realm stood higher. He had come to us in search of something, I thought. He officiated and preached a religion containing ancient elements, for my mother had told me that man's rituals had not changed much since her early days. But now here he stood, in his sanctuary, our sacred grove, seeking, perhaps within my mother's cavernous hollow trunk, the mystic centre without dimension.

The seven men gathered round him, in silence, as if in a trance, and the Arch-Druid, his eyes shut, his hands outstretched towards the leaden sky, the rain streaking down his forehead and cheeks, invoked: "O Ye, magical Fifth Fifth of the Five Fifths of the Island: Come to the Aid of my Powers, come to the Rescue of thy People, for a Wicked Magic has come from afar, and it threatens our Ancient Ways."

He stood on, speechless, motionless, till he felt the Power gathering about him. He felt the strength of his worship solidify, hardening into a solid force. Then he summoned that force into his inner being, and cast it forth.

When he returned to earthly things, he was different—wild-eyed like a wolf about to devour its prey, outspent and restless, altogether stunned. With this wild demeanour, the Arch-Druid was about to cut some leafy twigs from mother, as the other druid used to do. But he changed his mind, *and came to me*.

To be sure, mother's leaves were confined to her higher branches, therefore choosing me instead made sense. My lush foliage cascaded all the way to the ground. But how I wished, in those moments fraught with alarm, he had kept to my mother's, who was so accustomed to the ritual!

Not that a few twigs off me would make the slightest difference, but this man, what was he all about? Never before had I heard of the Fifth Fifth of the Five Fifths. It made for a fine tongue-twister, but what could it possibly mean?

As the druids left carrying away some green twigs of mine, I pondered about this extraordinary exploit from man, this puzzling creature. Never did I suspect, not for a moment, that it might bear some implications, or consequences, for us trees. It must be some new preposterous pastime of erratic, stumbling man, I concluded. I should have known better.

A few years before, somewhere many miles north of my forest, an undistinguished youth, abducted from native Britannia and made a slave here, had toiled as a shepherd until he had finally distinguished himself by escaping, both from slavery and from the Island. Years later, he had returned to the Island, this time as a freeman and with a mission. He had carried along a book. It was not just a book, which in itself was bound to appear as something almost supernatural, since the Island's humans were still a preliterate people. It was The Book, and it contained the Holy Scripture. And a new religion. His God-given mission was to divulge the new religion in my pagan Island.

"Pagan" was one more interesting imported concept. It did not mean that my Island's humans were irreligious. It meant that they worshipped false gods. As I had been inclined to smile when first introduced to manmade gods, I was once more amused to hear that those were not the *real* gods, and furthermore that the new, *real* thing was to be found in that Book.

The man who had returned to the Island of his captivity was one wholly devoid of rancour and rather filled with hope, confidence and optimism. Driven by an obsession which humans sometimes call a mission, he was the classic missionary man.

You may wonder how did I get to know this? As you may recall, Mother Nature had been sending over, since my very beginnings, all kinds of savants, go-betweens of knowledge. More often than not, such go-betweens had been insects, with the Knowing Cricket as their prototype.

I had not seen the Knowing Cricket for quite some time. Perhaps it had finally been squashed, or had really hopped away to some planet. But that is nothing whatever to the story I am telling.

My latest knowledgeable go-between was a slug. Not just *any* slug, of course, but a slender little thing with a mantle attractively sprinkled with neat cream dots. She claimed that she had come from a very distant land—and who didn't, among Mother Nature's itinerant lecturers? She now intended to rest

and graze on mother's algæ and lichens, which my mother did not
mind at all. Between the treecreepers and the Slug climbing up
and down her body, she was all atingle. The Slug was, despite her
supposed sluggishness, quite a spry microcosm. And with good
reason.

"There's so much I've got to tell you," she would say to me, "so
much, and such important things too!"

I couldn't wait, so I encouraged her by asking: "What exactly
were those druids doing here a fortnight ago?"

"Funny you should ask. That's precisely what's really
happening now all across the Island."

"How so?"

"The Arch-Druid and all druids are planning to meet with the
holy man to defeat his magic. They will use the leaves they took
from you and other noble yews throughout the Island in their
propitiatory rituals."

"The holy man," she had mentioned. So I asked her about him,
and she told me what I have told you.

This missionary man heralded a new religion in which he
believed to the point of having risked his life repeatedly in
divulging it among the Island's humans. Some of them had
proved hostile both to foreigners and to things foreign. Yet, the
holy man had journeyed far and wide, spreading the new faith
everywhere.

On one such journey, he came across a lovely meadow.
Thereabouts, he himself planted two yew trees, solemnly stating
that they were symbols of immortality. He was quite right in that.
The site became a town, which he named after us yew trees.

This was good news. It seemed as if, in respect to our worship,
he kept to the druidical custom which preached the doctrine of
immortality. But other than that, the new religion sounded
frightening.

I did not care about the holy man's claim that there was only
one God rather than a whole array of them. Or about his claim
that many humans had been "re-born in God" through him and a
ceremony which had to do with wetting women and men and
children too with water whilst he uttered magic phrases. I must
confess that I didn't grasp how these humans could possibly be

re-born when they hadn't died yet? I thought perhaps his magic was not that powerful. Besides, no matter how revolutionary his religion might be, he shared at least one feature with the local humans: a lingering fascination with heads. There had been, I must admit, a transition, and that was, from chopping heads off to counting them. How? His aim was to convert the maximum number of pagans, by the tens, the hundreds, the thousands. His mission almost amounted to a counting of heads. All of this, however, I did not particularly mind.

What I did mind was that his religion had come to him, and through him to our shores, from a nearly rainless and treeless land where, I feared, the emphasis hinged not on Mother Nature, but rather on her only gross error—man. Consequently, this religion was hostile to worship through nature, which in fact was portrayed as the kingdom of the devil.

"The devil?" I exclaimed in astonishment, only to find a sympathetic echo from the Slug.

"I know, it's absurd. You can ask your mother, me, or any other ancient being, and you'll always get a puzzled answer: 'The devil? It must be another human fabrication.'"

So the Spirit no longer lived in the woods, in the streams, in the skies. There was a book, instead, and the book, among other things, enjoined man to:

"Fill the earth, and subdue it: and have dominion over the fish in the sea, the birds in the air, and over every living thing that moves on earth."

Was the new religion going to seal the end of the sacred groves? Apparently, the one and only god was supposed to be worshipped in a one and only place, a temple, or church, which was made by human hands. How could that be?

I had never particularly liked the druids, though these men were some sort of a lesser evil when compared to the holy man. But the druids were losing the war they thought they could win. In that respect I do think he was gifted, for it still baffles me that one man alone—a book as his only weapon—could subjugate within his lifetime an ancient and strongly established religion.

"You should not be surprised," the Slug said one afternoon. It had taken her half the day to reach me, having come from my mother, who stood a few paces away. As a result of this prolonged trekking, she was hungry again, and just about to embark on the same voyage, in the opposite direction, back to my mother and the food she had for her. She gave me a concise explanation.

"Men go through cycles and sometimes, when they change a belief, or creed, there's no better explanation than this: they just tire of something, whatever it may be."

Towards the end of summer, the ash told us. The lofty pine and the other pines told us. Even the running hares—and foxes behind them—took time off their deadly chases to say: "Beware, the holy man is coming."

A plain-clothed, seemingly humble man walked through the woods, pacing calmly and praying all along. He stopped by us, caressed mother's gypsy roses, glanced round benignantly, and uttered: "Oh all ye green things upon the earth, bless ye the Lord; praise Him and magnify Him forever."

Forthwith, he cast a keener look on the shrubbery, spotted a small brown snake hiding in it, half-dead with fear, and said: "Come on out, ye little thing. Follow my steps."

Only much later did I come to know that this was the Island's last snake. The holy man had persuaded all the other ones to dive into the sea, so that at sea they may die by drowning. Present-day scientists affirm that the Island has always been snakeless, for a snake's fossil has never been found. Of course not! Snakes had always died at sea. It was their way to go. Not all at once, though. But the holy man cast them all off the Island. All but one. And this is what happened to it.

The missionary man banished it from the Serpent Lake in the Black Valley, where it had escaped and hidden. He put it in an iron box and said that he would let it out tomorrow. But tomorrow never came, and the Island was rid of snakes.

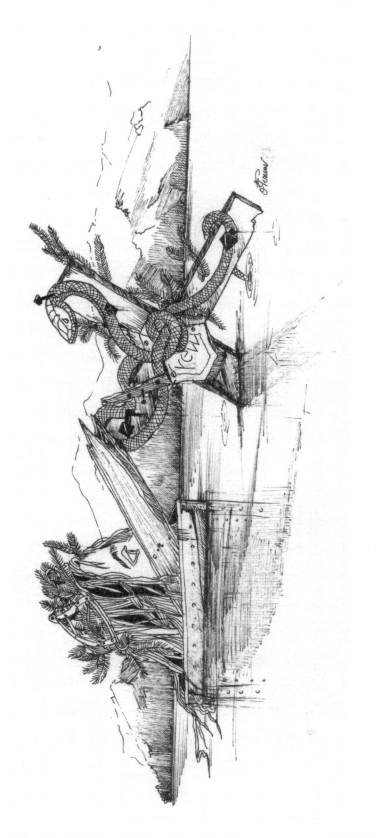

He put it in an iron box
and said that he would let it out tomorrow.
But tomorrow never came, and the land was rid of snakes.

SIX

Had I been of a more stubbornly single-minded temperament—the kind of temperament which often belongs to a male nature—I might have spent a thousand years entirely devoted to regret and self-mortification. As it was, I went into a profound state of self-induced dormancy. It was more than dormancy or deep sleep. It was a coma.

Present-day botanists state that our growth is anomalous. "It can occasionally accelerate, rather than decelerate, with age, and some trees show long periods of growth so minimal that any other species would have been dead within a couple of years." But then, most of humanity thinks of us as mere pumps, and cannot contemplate the possibility that we may act consciously. Yet, I had made the conscious decision to become unconscious.

I forced my younger roots to grow inwardly rather than outwardly, hoping that the resulting infilling might eventually choke me. Winter or summer, rain or shine, I stood there refusing to grow, refusing to live on, numb, comatose.

Why? Why, you may wonder? Because I hadn't paid attention, hadn't understood what had been manifest to everyone else in the woods. How could have I failed to see what was apparent? I, the Princess of the Forest, its privileged creature, predestined to reign over the species! Had I been blinded by all the attentions lavished on me by virtually every living thing on Earth, man included? Had I been deafened by the song of life and its enchantments? Or was it just petty vanity? How self-conceited had my beauty and youth made me? And, was it fair to blame it on youth? How many breezy afternoons and rainy mornings had I spent lost in admiration of my own greenness? Whilst I busied myself counting acorns or watching stars, talking to chirpy birds and fellow trees, marvelling at man's bizarre undertakings, my mother, my dear and just mother, was dying.

After so many springs and autumns, it is still painfully embarrassing to admit that I had no clue about her imminent death, whereas all the other "inferior" beings in the woods had understood only too well that it was coming.

Yet, all the clues were there. First and foremost, the appearance of that hideous bird—the treecreeper. It is the only bird that lives and feeds in standing carcasses of trees. Everything about it is suggestive of approaching death. It nestles where the dying tree's bark starts peeling away. It feeds on wood weevils and bark beetles, who in turn are taking advantage of the general state of decay. But I was green, so green... I had seen other trees decline and die, but they were our inferiors. Their destinies did not touch me, I thought. They were just part of Mother Nature's stew.

Then, if I would not question the sinister appearance of the treecreeper; the ever-increasing hollowness of my mother's trunk as opposed to the ever-decreasing amount of her living branches and leaves; if I would make nothing of the uncharacteristically respectful behaviour of gypsy roses, snakes, deer and many other animals and plants, how could I even remotely envision the massive attack of the natural predators of the forest—wood-boring insects and fungi? I know now that she was the victim of a relentless invasion of parasitic fungi. Millions of them, all obtaining their food from her rotting wood, with dampness and moisture as their staunchest allies.

And the fungal powers of reproduction are prodigious: millions and millions of them being born all the time, with a sole thing to accomplish—to suck life out of their victim.

For centuries, her crown had been making the foods to feed her roots, which, in turn, had used them to grow out so as to abstract the raw materials for the crown. Both her crown and her roots had been extending every year of her life. Her strongest branches and roots had extended the farthest, and her extremities had to be farther away every year from the trunk. Such extended lines of communication absorbed more energy just for the transport of her sap, and they couldn't but slow her growth.

Then, her sapstream had become more sluggish and her growth much less, slower and confined to the strongest shoots, while the weaker ones had withered and died back. That was her venerable senility.

A time had come when the distance from root-tip to branch-tip had become so great that the growth of both had ceased. Even the injury inflicted upon her by the windstorm had failed to produce durable re-growth. Only a hint of it, for my sake, I believe, so that she would be there, with me, as long as she could, to see me through all sorts of dangers. Poor mother!

The windstorm marked the beginning of her end. The numerous pests and diseases that had begun to take advantage of her weakened state found a wide-open door, and rushed in. Since then, there was tentative re-growth, tentative sprouting back, but no success, only decline. And then, her demise.

How could I have been so deaf as not to hear her cries? Perhaps she never did cry, perhaps she wanted to hide her dying, perhaps she did it all for me. But when I finally realised that she was gone and that I had been the last one to notice, I was stunned and grieved beyond what words can convey and what I felt I could endure.

Everything seemed revolting. I blamed myself, and found myself repugnant, for I perceived at long last that I ought to have been doing everything in my power to prevent her from dying. And not "just" dying, but dying in such a prolonged agony.

It was then that Mother Nature started to send me signals. This was not meant to be a time of grievance, but one of succession. I was the legitimate successor, as such I had been reared, and now the time had come to fulfil my obligation and become the Queen of the Forest. But my answer had been to go to sleep never to wake again. Life was no longer worth living.

Never would I have thought that there would be such a titanic struggle over a plant who simply refuses to live on. Every four or five years, as the strawberry tree told me, I gradually shed my leaves, and replaced them with new ones. Certainly, my formerly luxuriant foliage was gone. But, even though against my will, I managed to keep green. Meanwhile, the torpor continued.

One dewy morning, a strange rhythmic noise stirred me up. Still half asleep, I looked towards my mother. She was not there. Nothing was left, not a branch, not a twig, nothing. Only weeds growing where she had reigned for over a millennium. Fungi, bugs, rot, had been at work for years. What was left of her, of her long and just rule over the forest? Weeds.

In time, I overcame my disgust for weeds, for they really are herbs, and who is to say which is a weed and which is not? It was not just classism, though there was an element of that. It was that I loathed life and everything associated with it, let alone lowly weeds thriving on mother's remains.

I was ready to plunge back into my coma, but the annoying noise would not let me. Such a noise, regularly paced and metallic, was much unlike the woods and their animals, but very much like man. And in effect, there he was, one more representative of that proud species. The noise-maker was striking away at a bulky rock formation, about three times his height, doggedly, pauselessly.

To say that he appeared wild and woolly would be an understatement. Battling hair grew everywhere about his head, and fur—his fur?—all over the body. I wondered whether he was a bear? Had bears changed a bit since the last time I had seen them? Had they learned to use tools, such as the pickaxe he was swinging against the rock? But then I thought, "If that were a bear imitating man, he'd be better at it, for I don't recall ever seeing such a clumsy bear." (I did not know that by then the last bear had seen its last day on my Island.)

From time to time, the sequence of blows would be "Clang, Clang, Thud," then a pause, for the man's pickaxe was caught in an overhanging branch, or smashed into a harder stone, or, by missing its target altogether, sunk into the ground.

The pickaxing went on through the morning, and then well into the afternoon. It was almost dark when the man/bear, probably thinking it a good idea to finish the day's work on a high note, stepped back, balanced the pickaxe over his shoulders, and brought it down with a mighty blow. Instead of "Clang" or "Clank", all the woods heard a "THUD", and the pickaxe was torn into shreds. His reaction consisted of loud profanity, followed by immediate repentance, thus expressed: "O blessed be the Lord, Creator of all things. Thank You for Your punishment. Do lavish it upon me anytime you see fit."

Then I knew it was a man, for that was man's language and man's obsession: God. As for what he was doing in my forest, I had not the faintest clue.

Suddenly, I realised that I was wide-awake. The mourning, perhaps, was over.

I had to let my surviving roots and leaves know, and then start feeding them and myself again. It was time, my mother would have told me so herself.

Apart from restoring myself to life—which would have happened quite naturally and quite soon, for the spirit had not left me—I could count on the company of this entertaining man.

If I had finally succeeded in casting away my sorrow, the pines had not. One more distressing discovery was their disappearance. Having been totally unconscious when it happened, I could not shed any light on this mysterious occurrence, and my bosom friend, the strawberry tree, refused to tell me. At the time, I thought they had not been able to bear my mother's death; they might have all entered a state of self-imposed sleep, just like me. With one difference: a pine is no yew, and cannot take the same amount of abuse, by which I mean neglect.

I felt very sad. The pines had always been among mother's favourite subjects. Luckily, my sombre thoughts were driven off by the hermit's enterprises. I had found out why he spent day after day striking at solid rock. Through much toiling, he intended to turn it into a cave, in which to take shelter, as any hermit of repute. Pity there were no natural caves in my forest large enough to accommodate him, for he had been pickaxing for two moons, but with very little success. I could not say whether the rock was too hard or the metal head of his tool too soft, or both. Certainly, there had been little progress, but a tremendous waste of energy.

Sometimes I watched him carefully, and saw a weary man, frequently out of breath and ever out of context. If it was unperturbed contemplation that he sought, he had started off in the wrong direction, for I had never seen so dogged and yet so fruitless an endeavour. Where had he come from, and why?

In his younger years, he had lived somewhere on the Continent. He had left his mother and his eight sisters for the precise same reason his father had left years before—too many females in the house. A real house it could not be called. It was probably below standard even as a pigsty, and, perhaps, this accounted for the odd fact that the few pigs which were kept in there would periodically go missing. This constituted a disastrous economic leak for a household whose economy was anything but leakproof. The pigs were not bent on escapes or mysterious dematerialisations. Rather, the only man of the house was most bent on pigs. He utterly loved the taste of pork.

He ate so much of it, whenever he could lay his hands on a pig, that it must have gone to his head. So much so that one night he had a dream in which he saw a pig fluttering in the heavens, with golden wings, until it sat next to an angel on a puffy cloud. Interpreting this as a religious calling, the next morning he was on his way to a Benedictine monastery.

The abbot immediately realised how much more blissful his abbey would be without this loutish aspirant. One of the monastic rules, however, stated that the abbot would make no distinction of persons in the monastery, for all men are one in God. Reluctantly, the aspirant was accepted and set about his duties.

These were manifold and demanding, but at least one was to his liking. Between one set of prayers and the next, he was appointed herdsman of the monastery. He tended cattle, sheep and his beloved pigs. Not that he didn't pray at two a.m.; and then at dawn; then at six, nine, noon, three p.m., sunset and bedtime. Not that he didn't abide by the strict rules laid out by the monks, after having experienced in his youth riotous overindulgence, among other things in carnal pleasures. But he could not forget his dream. Blasphemous though it may seem, he could not help thinking that somehow there must be a relation between heaven and pigs. He was persuaded that the more pork he ate, the closer to salvation he got. Yet this was at odds with the rule that forbade eating the flesh of any four-footed beast. What to do?

To the astonishment of every monk in the abbey, all pigs began to limp. In time, they did away with one of their trotters. He had secretly and painstakingly trained them to do so. Then he pointed out that the pigs, having become three-legged, could be eaten with impunity.

The perplexed abbot made no objection, and the herdsman could have his favourite meal at all times. But his wrongdoing was discovered. He was put to shame and cast off.

Since then, he had wandered far and wide, crossed rivers, mountains and seas, becoming accustomed to a vagabond life and strange shelters. He had shared the beggar's blanket and crouched beside the sick and the castaway in many a nook and corner. Arrived on my Island, he had slept on bare heather, or in the ditch, with no roof over him but the vault of heaven. And it must have been during these frosty nights of unspoken terrors that, for the first time in his life, he felt something truly spiritual within his shivering bones, something he believed helped him through that darkness. This time, his resolve to become a religious recluse was genuine. When spring came, he headed for the wilderness and wended to my forest.

Eventually, he accepted his failure at digging a cave.

"It serves me right," he said, being in the habit of talking aloud to himself, "for I have been a sinner and God is now putting me through the Test."

That's how he resolved to live beneath me. Apart from speaking incessantly, in time he began to sing a song of which parts have survived down the ages. It is still remembered as The Hermit's Song.

> A hiding tuft, a green-barked yew tree
> Is my roof
> While nearby a great oak keeps me
> Tempest-proof.

The oak was *not* the one whose eighteen million acorns I had counted, but one of its offspring. By now, it had grown to a respectable size—larger than I was, though that did not matter, for its parent had been larger too, *once*. That was an uplifting note. I was just coming out of a devastating sense of loss and this one acorn out of eighteen millions who had actually come to something suggested that not all was in vain. And, if that was the oak in the song, I was the song's yew, and therefore the hermit's roof.

Not exactly a waterproof roof, as my foliage had thinned out considerably during the years of mourning. But what could the hermit care about a few raindrops? Or even about a night-time shower soaking him through? Wrapped in his sleeping furs, he slept like a log, and what did it matter if he woke sodden through and through and chilled to the bone? He had known greater hardships, and was determined to bear them all.

Life was not easy for him. At first he tried to trap small animals, such as hares. But his trapping skills matched the cave-digging ones. Then he thought he could *talk* to hares, and *invite* them to fall into his ill-devised traps. But no hare listened. Indeed, he was the one who had better listen, for one day he made nothing of some approaching growling and, the next thing he knew, he was climbing my trunk in great haste. A wolf pack was interested in his wildly scented flesh. My trunk was slippery, my lower branches had been shed—but the most daring wolf did get a taste of his skin. But no matter, no matter at all. Immersed in my foliage, sitting on a stout bough, he uttered: "O Lord Jesus Christ, Son of God, have mercy on me, a sinner."

Having said so, he felt inspired to kneel down to pray in the prescribed posture, forgot that he was up in the air, and took a crash dive against the limestone ground. A few minutes of rapture ensued, featuring the Celestial Vision of the Divine Light, and so on.

What kind of hermit was he? Wasn't he supposed not to be fond of talking? Why, he talked constantly, though he had no-one to talk to. Was he not supposed to say his prayers as frequently as he had when at the abbey, if not yet more frequently? Why, all he could remember and say was the one I have mentioned, "O Lord Jesus Christ, ... " And was he not at peace with himself after having renounced woman, children, wealth, fear of ridicule and the craving for social approval? I do not know about wealth, ridicule, social approval and what not, but I do know about his unrelinquished desire for a few things.

Sometimes, he would suddenly leap into the air, pull his hair and beard, run about in circles as if stunned beyond remedy, till he finally howled: "Pork! Have mercy on me and give me pork! OW!" Promptly stung by repentance, he would run to the lake and plunge into its cold waters.

Now and again, after a long day of frustrated attempts at various undertakings, he would lean against my trunk and sigh: "Woman..." and again, more loudly, "woman, woman, OW!" and dash off to the closest nettles. There, he would strip himself of his ill-smelling skins and plunge, stark-naked, into their stinging leaves.

After such a treatment, his complexion was redder than strawberries.

Was this what he had come here for? To achieve salvation through self-denial? Or, put bluntly, self-destruction? His personal salvation, his ascension from the realm of things, his union with his god had to go through these steps? Then his must be either an indifferent or a callous god indeed.

It was with great reluctance that I went to sleep, that autumn. He had provided seven moons of first-rate entertainment, and I wished I did not have to doze off just yet. Moreover, I was not too sure he would make it through the winter, which, according to what I had been told by many deer, could be harsh. It was a pity, but I had to go into dormancy. So, I wished him the best of luck, and slumbered off.

As soon as I reawakened, next spring, I looked round to see if he had survived. I did not need to look afield, for the hermit was nestling in my very branches, or, as I put it at the time, "on top of me!" I let out such a shriek that everyone in the woods roared with laughter. Admittedly, my reaction was far from queenly, but surprise had overwhelmed me.

Having been forced to rule out both cave and hut, the hermit had apparently opted for the proverbial pillar top. Save for the inconsequent detail that in my forest there were no manmade constructions.

The tree house had been built with posts, planks, branches and twigs from many different trees.

"There," I thought, "he's been at it again, making a mess out of everything he does."

But a juniper—a humble subject who hardly ever spoke—said: "Pray forgive me. I'm afraid you've overslept; you must have been tired. About a moon ago, when most of us were waking to early spring, there came a dreadful windstorm. It hit us with all its might and uprooted many trees, with my parents among them."

Poor thing, the first time I heard her say something it had to be about the loss of her parents. I certainly could feel sympathetic, and meant to let her know, but she continued: "I'm not looking for sympathy, though I appreciate it. I think you should know that, after the windstorm, the hermit walked all over the forest. He found the trees that lay on the ground, uprooted, lifeless, and dragged many logs back to you. That's why he has made the tree house with all kinds of woods."

That was puzzling. It would have been far simpler to select a few trees in my immediate proximity, fell them, and then build the house. And what of this eccentric house of his? It was, to put it mildly, eclectic, both in materials and style. Yet its thatched roof was waterproof, which was not for anyone to achieve. But here he

I did not need to look afield,
for the hermit was nestling in my branches.

came, I could feel his footsteps—and perceive at once that something was the matter.

Where was the two-legged animal who used to misstep his way through the woods? Not that he had become four-legged; but he was sure-footed, at ease in the woods, more so than any human I'd ever seen. What had become of his bearlike demeanour? No more furs about his body, but a plain woollen cloak instead. He was singing his tune and here too there was improvement. Though he was no song thrush, his intonation and delivery were a far cry from his former groaning.

> I can pick my fruit from an apple
> Like an inn,
> Or can fill my fist where hazels
> Shut me in.
>
> A clear lake beside me offers
> Best of drink,
> And there grows a bed of cresses
> Near its brink.

There was no doubt: the man had changed.

Bewitching days and nights came to pass. I could feel that something was afoot, something extraordinary. This bony man who had been little more than a clown, this man had stopped praying altogether, having come to recognise that every stone, raindrop, and sun ray breathed prayers. He did not look so much towards the sky, but rather kept his eyes and wits about him. He had kind words for the woods in general and for me, his landlady, in particular.

These were not the words of a fool. He began to call me the Tree of Knowledge, and there was little flattery in this, only truth. He did eat fish or meat, sometimes, just as the wolf pack would have eventually eaten him alive had he kept sleeping beneath me, defenceless at their mercy.

Summer came, and he added summery lyrics to his song.

And when the summer spreads its mantle
What a sight!
Marjoram and leeks and pignuts,
Juicy, bright.

He did not behave the way I had seen man behave, nor did he behave like any of the other lowly beasts. I must confess I could not sort him out.

One early autumn afternoon, he kindled a small fire in the hearth of the tree house. Next, he went to the lake to fetch some water, which he placed, in a kettle, on top of the fire. Then he plucked a few berries and leaves from my boughs. When the water boiled, he poured it in a cup in which he steeped my leaves, so as to make a brew. On a rugged wooden dish he laid my berries. Then he sat down to his supper, serenely.

I remember as if it had happened yesterday. He ate my berries one by one, crunching and then swallowing their poisonous seeds too. Then he brought the just as deadly brew to his lips and drank it. Finally, *he looked at me.* Had I had eyes, they would have fallen at his steady gaze. He spoke.

"I know you can hear me. *But I can hear you too.*"

As I observed him, startled and bewildered by the revelation, for no man had ever been able either to speak or to understand our language, I noticed that some leaves covered part of his face, as if they grew on it.

The last time I saw him, shortly before winter, he had leaves growing all over his body. They were now his only clothes.

Since then, he has wandered across many islands and lands. Centuries later, man built great places of worship—cathedrals— to celebrate his gods. Their soaring columns and arched roofs resembled the trunks and vaultlike canopies of sacred groves, such as mine. Vegetation poured forth from everywhere. Amidst such vegetation, again and again, there lies, carved out of the stone, the leafy face of the Green Man.

SEVEN

In spite of my prolonged coma, and of thirty years of suicidal tendencies, I was alive. I knew it only too well. My photosynthesis was as efficient as ever in capturing sunlight and synthesising organic and inorganic elements into energy, which I stored in the sweetest sugar molecules. My leaves' chlorophyll was greener than the greenest grass. My cells kept dividing, enlarging and differentiating at such a pace that I began to wonder if my growth could be indefinite. My metabolism ran smoothly; fungi and pests could not attack me; and man, the greatest danger, had chosen to make yews relevant once more in his new religion, as a symbol both of immortality and of death.

By associating my being evergreen and my longevity with immortality, man had begun to plant yews in the immediate proximity of his new places of worship, by now wholly manmade—churches. Either in the churchyard or by the graveyard grew a "sombre" and "pensive" yew tree. This made for almost ensured survival.

However, during my protracted mourning, alarming things had happened, and alarming reports from trees and, lately, even from animals, had reached me. The Green Man had diverted my attention from them, but only temporarily. Anxiety had swept the woods. I could no longer indulge in my sorrow and remorse; no longer seek diversions. Ultimately, I could no longer idle. By taking on my mother's legacy, I had to shoulder, so to speak, all the responsibilities connected with leadership. There was no other legitimate or natural pretender.

Had I not become the leader of the forest, someone else would have. And I intuitively knew that no-one could carry out the queen's duties better than I would. By then, I was not only the oldest tree of any species in the forest but a true matriarch. Dozens and dozens of my offspring had been growing steadily for decades, some even for a few centuries. Not only did I have all the qualifications as a direct successor to my mother—I had an obligation to do what I had been conceived to do. What sense would it have made to abdicate to one of my offspring? Now that kindred-and-not trees were coming to me pleading for help, how could I fail them?

Yet, I would have. I must confess that I did not care to take command. I would have gladly handed it over, so to speak, to a son of mine. A son rather than a daughter for I had noticed, down the centuries, that the male nature craves power more than the female. Nevertheless, if I finally yielded to my obligation, it is because I reasoned in a quintessentially feminine way.

First, I was a mother; and then, a matriarch. Even for us yews life can be difficult. Of the millions and millions of arils—my berries containing one seed each—only a few had sprouted. Fewer yet had become trees. It was up to me to protect the surviving ones, just as my mother had protected me. Therefore, with the most steadfast determination that exists—a loving mother's—I took on absolute leadership, and declared war. On whom?

Do you recall my mother's words, when I was a seedling and she explained the hierarchy of the forest?

"Among the leaf-shedding trees there are two giants: the mighty Oak and the daring Ash."

The ash had proved a loyal subject. Only a few ashes had remained in the woods, and, thanks to their height, they were our sentinels and lightning rods.

The oaks had taken a different path. There were very many of them, and, as my mother had put it, they were all "powerful and ambitious." That explained the "skirmishes" the yews had had with them over the millennia. But the present threat was no skirmish. The oaks had been waging a guerrilla warfare all through my long sleep; by ridding the forest of all other species, they were attempting to take it over and turn it into a pure oak grove.

This was not leadership, of course, but dictatorship, whereas my role implied ruling the forest and *all* its species in the interest of them all, not just of the yews. (If I say so in this context but then history shall contradict me, it is because I want you to know that even for an age-old yew there arise situations beyond her control.)

Next came a purely strategic concern: how would I wage a war? Was I to let the oaks plainly know that most living beings in the woods, plants and animals alike, despised them and did not want them to triumph? I was no strategist, no warlord, or better "warlady", but I had intuition. While I realised that a direct confrontation would be suicidal, I also suspected that victory might be gained by surprise. My military operation would involve deception. Yes, you heard me, deception.

You may recall a much younger and greener little tree say that "we cannot lie, and we always tell the white and shining truth." Indeed, my mother herself lied to me when she assured me that she was well, but her lying was different from just any lying. She knew, of course, how ill she really was, but had repressed her knowledge into her unconscious while holding in her consciousness ideas better suited to her aim, and that was, hiding the truth of her illness from me. That was deception at its noblest level. Mine would be that greasy contrivance which lubricates so many mundane transactions.

Deception meant to appear to be incompetent even though I was competent. To appear to be ineffective, though I was effective. I was to wait for the oaks to be on the point of making their final move, their massive attack. Then I would feign to be cowed, so as to raise their spirits. I would give the appearance of inferiority and weakness, to make them proud, and boastful, and imprudent. Well, hadn't I done just that? My attempted suicide first. Then my reluctance to take command. Finally my interest in farcical human activities. All these told of a general state of weakness. The oaks could not suspect my sudden, if tardy, turnabout. And that was to my advantage. So I let them be under the impression that they were superior and that my forest could be taken easily. Meanwhile, I developed a secret plan of action.

The days of that memorable summer grew shorter, until autumn came and the oaks, having shed all their leaves, went to sleep. Only when they were fast asleep did I summon the Council of War.

I was not keen on words such as "warlord", "council of war", etc. I find them crude and unfeminine. In their stead, I adopted the terms "leader", for myself, and, for the Council of War, "The Evergreen Club". Which was made up of my bosom friend the strawberry tree, the humble juniper, and a most beautiful holly tree whom I have never mentioned before because of... jealousy.

She was, and had been for two hundred years, a splendid tree, with wonderfully glossy leaves and the brightest red berries. At the height of my vanity I had come to fear that she might be deemed prettier than I was. Now that matters were a trifle more pressing, I had no time to worry about beauty contests, and needed her help.

We evergreens go to sleep later than the oaks, about a month later, and wake about a month earlier. Therefore, we could count on two months—one well into autumn, the other shortly before and during early spring—in which we were wide-awake and active whilst our enemies were sleeping soundly. This was an exceptional advantage, one which we must exploit.

The first formal meeting of The Evergreen Club is a milestone in the war's chronicle. It was a nippy morning in early winter. The strawberry tree, basking in the pale wintry sun with clusters of both fruits and flowers hanging from its branches, had, at my behest, summoned all the members. The meeting was held in great secrecy. All the leaf-shedding trees were fast asleep, and there weren't many animals or insects about. Nevertheless, the talks resembled a peculiar exercise in "hush hush, whisper whisper". The humble juniper spoke first.

"Honourable Members of the Club," she said, the same gentle creature I had got to know better since my mother's death, "I'm afraid that first of all we should assess how many casualties we have suffered. According to my latest estimate, the number of casualties is staggering. If we take the Queen Mother's death as the date of commencement of the hostilities, thirty-three years ago, then we have lost:

76 birches;
84 alders;
45 willows."

After a mournful pause, she resumed: "Some of them might have been already on their way out, since they are all short-lived species, but the oaks unquestionably accelerated the process. When it comes to cherries, crab apples, hawthorns and rowans, my estimate can only be tentative. Cumulatively, we have lost two, maybe even three hundred of them. As for the stately pines, I think they were all wiped out by the oaks. The noble hollies suffered some casualties, as we know. We junipers haven't quite yet, and not because we haven't been attacked, but simply because we are so frugal by nature that we can survive on scrap, so to speak. Naturally, we'd prefer to live and to thrive rather than barely to get by. The strawberry trees have not been attacked yet, merely as a result of their being all situated along the forest's edges."

"And pray tell me," I broke in, quite anxiously, "what of my offspring?"

I should have known. An embarrassed pause followed, then she said: "I regret to report that a dozen of your daughters and sons have perished under the direct attack of the oaks."

All members were respectfully silent as I grappled with the reality. The strawberry tree suggested: "The younger yews seem to have been their primary target, among the noble evergreens. To... hem... kill a yew, it takes the oaks ten to twenty times what it takes them to do away with a willow, or an alder. But I think they have done so in order to test their power. They realise that the final struggle will be fought between many oaks and a few indomitable yews. They took advantage of your 'absence' to... train against the yews."

"Their strategy is twofold:" the juniper defined precisely, as was her tidy habit, "they either shade out young saplings or low trees with their spreading branches, letting nearly no light through their leaves; or they send out girdling roots that kill the roots of the other nearby trees by growing about them and squeezing the cambium to death. A simple strategy, but an effective one, unfortunately."

That was enough, I thought. But not quite.

"Lastly," the holly added, "we have begun to lose some birds. They no longer dwell here because the habitat has been changing and they don't like the new one."

We all could appreciate how important birds were. Apart from keeping us cheerful with their chatter and happy with their singing, they kept us clean and scattered our seeds.

We spent the rest of the day discussing several strategies and agreed to convene again in a few days so as to decide which forces to use in our counterattack, and when to mobilise them.

The next time we met it was raining so overwhelmingly that we did not have to whisper any longer, but rather shout. That was, of course, irritating to me, both because it did not behoove a queen and because there was little chance to get into strategic assessments when we could barely hear one another. I did manage to hear the holly say something akin to: "I gave the whole matter much thought, and have concluded that our best tactic against the oaks lies in their mechanical removal."

"In their what?" the strawberry tree asked.

"Why, in their mechanical removal. You know, toppling them over, blowing them off... that sort of thing."

"That's brilliant," I said, or rather shouted. "And how do you propose we achieve their 'mechanical removal'?"

The holly looked perplexed, and mumbled something, which she then had to repeat by screaming: "Well, the details need to be worked out. Surely, our friend the juniper can sort it all out. But it is a clever plan, isn't it?"

Obviously, removing the oaks would rid us of the problem altogether. But we could not do it. We are not possessed of the cataclysmic power of destruction with which mankind has shown itself to be so generously endowed.

I remember being relieved by the holly's clumsy suggestion. Beautiful though she was, her thinking was that of a reed at best, and I understood then that I did not have anything to fear from the hollies. I, on the other hand, had been involved in some more substantial thinking, and had come up with a composite plan.

A political campaign preceded the military one. Much convincing was in order if I wanted to gain the support of many allies, indeed as many as I could get. Consequently, I had the junipers within and without the forest summon the animals I needed to harangue. In a few days, thousands of blue tits, red squirrels, and red deer were fluttering, leaping, trotting about me, having promptly answered their queen's summons.

Earlier on, towards the end of summer, I had asked a cuckoo to detour from her usual route back to her winter quarters so as to drop by on the larger island across the sea, towards the rising sun. There, she was supposed to ask the local woodpeckers to pay me a visit at their earliest convenience, and I stressed "earliest". As it turned out, she complied most courteously to my request. I wonder why? What was in it for her? Not much, really. But cuckoos are unconventional, eccentric birds. I planned to have a long talk with all the moths-to-be early next spring.

Now, with winter approaching, I had to persuade the disorderly assembly to do as I said. These were animals, simple, lowly beings. In order to appeal to them, I had to show them what they would get in return for their alliance. I said: "Survival is the name of the game, the most common attractor on Earth."

I do not know if they could relate to that "attractor" notion, but I could see how well they appreciated attraction. The deer's rut was under way just then, and the stags roared and groaned incessantly, so as to *attract*, precisely, the doe. The squirrels were after acorns just like the tits were after bugs. Sexual drive and hunger were magnets, and it was evident to everyone that survival was essential to existence. I resumed: "In time, all systems must fail."

This they did not grasp. I could tell because they gave me a baffled stare. Their attention span being what it was, I had to get to the point.

"What you all must do is give the advantage to the tree that will outlive the others, and will supervise all the changes. The fittest trees for you are the large, old trees that are sound except for a few, well taken care of cavities. Compared to me, or to a holly, or a to a strawberry tree, an oak is a youngster." They laughed. I pressed on. "Any ignorant animal, man included, can be greedy and take everything."

I felt that this had *not* gone down well, but at risk of taking an unpopular stand, I must make them see farther away than short-sighted, hot-blooded beings usually see. "The saying, 'The more, the better' in the long run can only bring about harm. I, on the contrary, *will* discriminate, sort out what it is that the forest needs, as a community, keeping *all* its dwellers in mind. No organism can live in perfect solitude, much less so a large, long-lived tree. To get too much, too fast, too soon, is ultimately self-destructive. A forest made up solely of oaks would be out of control. A more varied forest affords a more varied food web."

"A *what?*" they asked. By now I had their attention, and had better not let go of it.

"What I mean is that the more variety, the more foods, the more animals, and vice versa. There must be a sharing of power. Finally, you all fear man, don't you?" They certainly did. "Then let it be known that man's new religion holds us yews in high esteem, just like the old religion. I am this Island's Queen, and you must understand that queens and kings have to endure, for the sake of stability and for the overall fitness of things." (Goodness gracious: I was beginning to sound like mother!)

The speech was well received and digested forthwith. Deer, squirrels and blue tits assured me that I could count on their vast populations. I explained to them, in detail, what I expected them to do.

Winter went by smoothly and mildly; in fact, quite mildly. Yews are only partially dormant in winter. In my woods, most evergreens were fully asleep, for, as the holly put it, "There's nothing like sleeping through winter." But, having grown older and more experienced, I had mastered the art of dozing on and off according to temperature and, mind you, to my will. Therefore, I had been able to keep an eye, so to speak, on the work of my allies.

As planned, most blue tits had left the forest. This was unprecedented. Before their long sleep, the squirrels had disposed of the oaks' acorns as I had told them. Finally, hundreds and hundreds of deer had made, of the soil about the oaks, their favourite stamping grounds.

Sometimes, shortly after midday, the temperature was mild enough to allow me to wake, albeit briefly. Then I saw them at work. Mighty stags and elegant does, and even their calves, kept circling round our enemies, treading, tramping, stamping on the soil beneath them. The oaks were fast asleep, wholly unaware of the thousands of hoofs grinding over their roots relentlessly. It was a sight to behold! But I alone saw it happen, for man was elsewhere and otherwise engaged, and my fellow evergreens had not yet mastered the art of sleeping more or less at will. At any rate, everything was proceeding according to my strategy.

Shortly before spring, all the members of the Evergreen Club were awake and agog with anticipation. Gently, but firmly, I had to forbid my suitors—many a male yew—from sending over their clouds of pollen. Clearly, this was not a time for lovemaking, but one for war. As the oaks were still asleep, and knowing they would not reawaken for one more moon, I took my time and made my moves with queenly aplomb.

First I spoke to the moths-to-be, truly inferior beings which I would have much rather shunned. But wartime calls for compromises, and this was one. I simply said: "All I'm asking you to do is what you do best—devour oak leaves. This year, thanks to your Queen's noble-mindedness, you will be able to go about your devouring business *without* any danger from the blue tits."

I was somewhat bluffing. I did not know for sure whether or not my "exchange programme" would work. At any rate, the moths-to-be believed me, or at least did not reply, and, since silence gives consent, I considered them as more allies of mine.

Thereupon it was the woodpeckers' turn. That would be a thornier negotiation, for we trees have a very special relationship with birds and, though I would certainly not think of them as equals, I refrained from ordering them about as if they were mindless moths. I asked my bosom friend, the strawberry tree by the lakeside, to negotiate with them on my behalf. It is embarrassing to confess that one of my favourite suitors would not hear of holding back his seasonal courtship. Would you think me unforgivably frivolous if I confessed that, exceptionally, I devoted some time to lovemaking?

The strawberry tree had managed to retain some of its fruits on its branches. They were all past their prime, and more insipid than usual, but the woodpeckers, who had never tasted them or seen them before in their forest, found them delightful. Answering the invitation I had forwarded to them through the cuckoo, a delegation of high-ranking woodpeckers had arrived from the island across the sea. The strawberry tree was to persuade them to migrate to our woods along with their population and spend the summer here. There were no woodpeckers on my Island, there never had been any. Consequently, the different bugs residing in the barks of many, many trees had never known their bill, against which they would prove totally unprepared. (I had another use for their bills in mind, but I first had to lure them into coming.)

"You see," the strawberry tree told their leader, a fetching female specimen who had taken her perch on a high branch and hardly ever left it, "our woods abound with tens of thousands of bugs who believe they are untouchable because there is no bird in these woods whose bill can poke through a tree's bark."

But it's not easy to negotiate with birds; they are so inherently flighty.

The strawberry tree, host to the woodpeckers' delegation, was all atwitter, day in, day out. Soon the oaks would reawaken; one way or the other, the negotiation must be concluded.

"So," the strawberry tree asked on an early spring day, addressing itself to the female leader in the friendliest manner, "what do you think?"

"I think this is a miserably rainy spot, that's what I think. Where we come from," she continued, "it doesn't rain so much. When our feathers get sodden through and through, we can't fly."

Dreadful news, but the strawberry tree commented: "Why, you won't need to fly that often; most trees here can feed one of you for weeks. Besides, think how shiny your plumage will be. You will be gorgeous!"

"Am I not already?"

"Yes, of course. But the shine will enhance your beauty and make you look as you never have before."

This still did not seem to persuade her. What eventually did was the beautiful view she could behold from the strawberry tree.

"I love this vista," I heard her sigh one day.

"Vista" sounded like a man's word, and a man from distant lands at that. I assumed that she must have travelled extensively, and suspected that our lake reminded her of other lakes where she had dwelled. Eventually, she agreed to return, with her population, just before summer.

As soon as she flew off into an unusually clear sky, I summoned the blue tits. I could be more straightforward with them, as we had been friends for centuries.

"When the woodpeckers get here, a few moons from now," I said, "you will all fly away at once and go live in their forest, just for the summer. It's an... exchange programme. It'll be mutually beneficial."

They agreed, right away. Birds are nature's explorers and geographers. Even non-migratory birds love an occasional change of air.

And now, the showdown.

Soon, it was a matter of days, maybe just a couple of days, before I would say, to the reawakening oak closest to me, "Hello, hello. How are you? Did you sleep well?"

"Yes, thank you," answered a giant oak a few paces away from me, one that had been trying to shade me out for fifty years or more. "I slept very well. And how are *you*, Queen of the Forest?"

"Not too well. I'm afraid I am rather unwell."

"Oh, I'm sorry to hear that. Surely, it is nothing serious?"

The truth, of course, was quite the opposite. I was as healthy as ever, for we yews are champion shade-bearers, and the oak's attempts at shading me to death left me indifferent. It was the oak who was suffering. Thousands of hoofs had tramped for months over her roots. The deer had thus compacted the top layer of the soil, and the roots had begun to die, for lack of oxygen and water alike. I must admit that I was barbarously taking pleasure in my enemy's tribulation. It pretended to feel fine, when it felt rotten; I complained about the poor state of my health, when in fact I had been engineering a mass murder, and this oak was one of my many victims. And it was not the only one to reawaken in bad shape and worse spirits. The woods resounded with the oaks' suffering.

The members of the Evergreen Club gathered the news, even from the blooming violets and primroses. The oaks had been taken ill. It was my first success in the war. But we absolutely must keep up the deception. Therefore, I had suspended the deer's traffic before the first oak reawakened out of its slumber.

Within a month, the oaks were better. The rain, never in short supply here, helped them by softening the soil to a certain extent and giving back water. Eventually, some oxygen too found its way to the roots. They were not as strong as they used to be, and conceivably they would not be able to wage war that summer. Still, they were far from dead. It was time to launch my second offensive.

As millions of moth caterpillars came into being, in May, they immediately started to devour oak leaves, as voraciously as ever. More than ever, since their natural enemies, the birds that would eat an average of one hundred and fifty caterpillars a day, were nowhere to be found. My loyal blue tits had migrated en masse to the neighbouring island as soon as an immense flock of outlandish-looking birds had arrived in my forest. It was the exchange programme. It was my deadliest weapon.

According to my instructions, the woodpeckers confined their activities to the oaks. First, they drilled hundreds of holes in living oaks so as to make their nests. Then they began to peck the trunks in a circle till they girdled the trees. And they continued to peck in search of insects, particularly ants, which, mixed with inner bark and sap, they fed to their young. As previously noted, the blue tits were conspicuously missing, and the caterpillars could thrive and eat incessantly without being eaten, at least by them. In short, a tree's nightmare, one from which the oaks could not awake.

I had feared a counterattack, but the oaks were defenceless and incapable of reorganising their devastated ranks, let alone taking the offensive. Here and there, an oak managed to strangle a birch sapling or a small cherry tree. That was all.

By midsummer, the oaks, virtually entirely defoliated, put out a new crop of leaves, as was their custom. Even today I am at a loss when attempting to understand exactly where they got the energy required for a new crop in such terribly deprived conditions. My plan came to an unforeseen halt.

The new leaves contained high levels of tannin which made them less palatable to the caterpillars. After having suffered the raging attacks of my divisions, I had speculated that the oaks would never get to that stage. Wrongly.

"The caterpillars are not eating them, they aren't eating the leaves anymore!" the holly shouted. And that was not all. The woodpeckers were finding their toil increasingly futile. Why should they peck into hardwood to extract insects when they had millions of clumsy caterpillars at the mercy of their bills?

"A major setback," the strawberry tree commented when summer had been over for a moon. The juniper had been calculating all along, and was now ready to produce the results.

"Some oaks, in fact quite a number of them, 37, have died. At least 200 are in very bad shape. And close to 50 quite out of sorts. But we have not succeeded entirely. They have not been wiped out."

"At least they'll have no offspring, this time," broke in another juniper.

That was true. The previous autumn, I had made the squirrels carefully dispose of the oaks' acorns in a way that would prevent them from being born. Still, we were far from victory, and by now the oaks knew that we were after them.

That winter the deer did what they had done the previous winter. They stamped over the oaks' soil, but with less vigour, for less time, and in smaller numbers. As for the woodpeckers, I sent them back to their island telling them never to come back again (that is why there are no woodpeckers on my Island). The blue tits returned and, in spite of my requests, could not refrain from eating tens of thousands of caterpillars.

In short, we had reached not a truce, for neither party had any intention of coming to terms with the other, but a stalemate. The oaks which had been girdled and had not yet died, eventually did die. Their number and power had decreased, but I still was not the unchallenged Queen of the Forest. And it was evident that, although we were winning the war, to continue it for a long time would blunt our edge and dull our forces. Indeed, something of the sort had already happened to some of my allies.

A dull war dragged on for longer than a long-lived man's life, and then that of his son, and the son of his son. No decisive battles, not enough casualties to tilt the balance of power further in my favour. What to do?

By then I had seen over eight hundred springs. I was more myself, though I did not sense that I *knew* myself more, by which I mean better, more deeply. But I had always felt that vulnerability was in my opponents, invincibility in myself. I had seen them perish under my attacks; I had seen them rot and collapse to the ground, where they rotted further, until nothing was left of them. And at best, the oaks would not exceed a lifetime of three, four hundred springs. Why could I live for so much longer? There had to be something more, something other than ordinary knowledge stored away somewhere amid my cells.

I withdrew from the society of other trees and spent most of my time thinking, in great secrecy, particularly whilst the other trees slept, including those from the Evergreen Club. I suspected that something was bound to turn up only if I thought about it unceasingly. Eventually, I came to understand that many growth phenomena which I had previously deemed automatic and taken for granted, could be tampered with, even wilfully directed. All I had to do was take control of some chemical substances produced by most trees in minute amounts, which I shall call growth regulators. Actually, since my intentions were destructive and not constructive, I concentrated on growth *inhibitors*.

In time, I mastered the art of producing such substances at will, and tested them on the oak which stood nearby. Beginning in the early spring of a memorable year, I exuded fairly large quantities of growth-inhibiting substances in my immediate surroundings. These were supposed to bring about the onset of the senescent phase—or the ageing process—of a plant, and hasten it until it killed the plant altogether. Was it going to work?

I kept at it for three moons, and then I had the answer. One late spring evening, shortly before dusk, the mighty oak gave me a wintry stare, so to speak. The forest grew silent.

"You are killing me!" it said.

Indeed, I *was*. But, in the process, I had been killing a few innocent onlookers—a rowan, some ivy, even a lofty ash. The weapon worked, but I had to perfect it, so as to be able to kill selectively.

I spent a few decades refining the skill and teaching it to my offspring, since it had become evident that only we yews could deal with such powerful instruments of destruction. My daughters and sons eventually learnt, and, at long last, I had a reliable army.

When we launched our great offensive, one could almost feel the growth inhibitors run amok in a frenzy to kill. For a while I feared that we might overkill the woods, and when my fear became a reality, it was too late to stop the substances we ourselves had been releasing.

These proved to be still too powerful, especially when unleashed in such large quantities and all at once. Alas, we killed many of our friends and allies and even some evergreens. The oaks were devastated, but not entirely wiped out. I did not dare insist, lest my offspring and I should kill every plant in the woods.

Then Mother Nature, or simply my own overexcited sensitivity, sent me one last messenger.

"Take heed of the fungi which live with the oaks' roots," I was told. "Learn about them, and then devise a way to upset this relationship."

These were the mycorrhizal fungi. They lived in symbiosis with the non-woody, absorbing roots of the oaks. Many trees are dependent on this fungus-root association of mutual benefit, and the oaks particularly so, while we yews can do with and without them, indifferently. In essence, a delicate balance between host plant, in this instance the oaks, and symbiont, the mycorrhizal fungi, resulted in enhanced mineral absorption for each member. It was my task to alter this association.

Resorting to powers I never thought I could employ, the sort of powers known only to an elite of trees on Earth, I commenced a new phase of the war.

At the time of the oaks' root shedding, I was able to discourage the formation of the root protection at the base of the dying roots. Without such a protection, the friend of yesterday became the foe of today. The fungi turned on the oak trees and began to digest the non-woody roots. The oaks put up a desperate fight, but they were on the road to death, and, after the dysfunction I had caused reached a threshold, there was no return.

One by one, within the next few years I saw them come crashing down to the ground. Mighty oaks they had been, dangerous and rebellious enemies too; but I had turned them into scrawny stumps, at first, and then into rotting logs, lying lifeless on the stony ground of my forest.

All were gone but two young oaks. They knew that there was no place for them in my new order of the woods, yet pleaded to have some of their acorns sown somewhere else, so as to avoid extinction. I was moved to clemency, and granted the two oaks their boon. I summoned the squirrels and ordered them to collect all the acorns they could find. Then they must leave our peninsula and reach across the lake, there to sow all the acorns, which they were strictly forbidden to eat. They obeyed me. Everyone had become more eager to obey me since my deadly display of brute force.

Today one can behold a wonderful oak grove, along the lake's shores, across from us. Such oaks are the descendants of the ones I permanently removed from my woods.

There I was, the High Queen of the Forest. I had made a clean sweep of our enemies, and stood my ground proudly.

More ventilated, more in the sun, with more soil at my disposal, I could avoid what had happened to my mother, and that is, to be enfolded by the choking embrace of too many trees, shrubs, weeds, mosses, lichens, algae, fungi, bugs, shade, dampness, and rot. Meanwhile, I was clearing the way for my

Mighty oaks they had been, dangerous and rebellious enemies too;
but I had turned them into scrawny stumps, at first,
and then into rotting logs
lying lifeless on the stony ground of my forest.

daughters and sons to come to me, for they were close but still not in sight. I do not think I was loved, as my mother had been. I believe I was feared. Even the strawberry tree seemed to be intimidated.

I had recently turned a thousand springs old. It was then that I heard news of that puzzling species, mankind, which had deserted my woods for quite some time. An obscure chieftain born not far from my forest, one Brian Ború, had succeeded in doing away with kings and kinglets. After many wars and usurpations, there was finally a High King who had unified the Island under his rule.

But the High King was soon killed on the battlefield, and his shaky complex of alliances broke up again.

I, on the contrary, remained the undisputed Queen of the Forest. High, and dry, and lonely.

EIGHT

There was once, many springs ago, a cottage by the sea. It stood atop a rocky cliff, and by its entrance grew a yew tree who told me what I am about to tell you.

In that damp and smoky cottage dwelled a fisherman, his young wife and their baby girl. One night, as the baby slept in the crib, the mother was weeping. Her man was still out at sea, and the storm was swelling round those rocky cliffs. The woman would cry, "Oh, husband dear, come back to us."

She gazed at their slumbering creature as she numbered her beads, and smiled at her as the baby smiled in her sleep.

"Bless you, bless you, my darling. I know that angels are watching over you. I know they're whispering with you, and keeping bright watch over your sleep. Oh, pray to them, my baby, pray to them softly. Tell them you'd rather they'd watch over your father, for you're safe here with me, but he's lost, out there, in the wrath of the raging sea."

Hopeful prayers lived through the stormy night till morning came. Dawn and calm returned along with the fisherman. The wife wept with joy when she saw her baby's father, and, caressing her child, whispered: "I knew that angels were watching over you."

The windblown and gnarled yewess who told me this story never had the chance, in her life of hardships, to receive pollen from a male yew tree. She had never been a wife, never a mother. So, she could not possibly understand the meaning of love. *I* could.

The fisherman was numb with cold, bruised and weary. His wife boiled water over the hearth, and then mixed it with cold water to rub her husband's body with a woollen cloth soaked in the mix. The man fell asleep. He slept all day whilst the woman tended to their baby girl.

When night fell and the baby slumbered off, her father woke. The day was spent and the stars, far asunder, twinkled as keenly as they do on a frosty night. Forgetful of the perils of the previous night, of the wrecked fishing boat, of the bleak prospects that, boatless, lay ahead for his family, he drew near his wife. Without exchanging words, man and woman kissed, embraced, and made love, their bodies entwined, their attention undivided. Both she and he willing to give everything to each other, they kissed and prayed, a thanksgiving prayer, as their lungs breathed with the night and heaved with the waves down below the cliffs.

Their loving and praying unfolded under the starry sky as an assertion of life, and the woman and the man felt like one.

Likewise, for over two hundred springs since the ending of the war, two yew trees, a female and a male, had been growing side by side, not far from where I stood. They were not my offspring. They thrived, happy and undisturbed, in the forest that we had ridden of our competitors. Towards the end of every winter, just after our yearly reawakening, the male yew released clouds of pollen which were wind-borne for a mere instant, as they immediately alighted on his wife. She welcomed them all, wasted none, and asked for more until the season ended. In autumn, she bore the loveliest berries.

Lucky them to have been born but a few paces from one another, their leafy fronds intermingling and overlapping in a cascade of two different hues of green, the female's darker, the male's lighter. They stood in an unending embrace, and, their trunks almost hidden behind their bountiful foliage which reached to the ground, one could have thought it was a single tree, surmounted by an immense crown.

This was love. This was what I did not have and craved after centuries of war and alienating leadership. During the last phase of the war, I had forced myself not to bloom at all. I had succeeded, and in the end I was the unchallenged queen. But *so* unloved.

In many centuries, I had seen copulation as it occurs in the animal kingdom, and it had struck me as a rather tempestuous affair, in which badgers, boars, wolves and what have you went about one another with much purring, groaning, panting and so on. I had always found it rather unbecoming, but then, was that not what animals were, as opposed to us stately trees? Yet, women and men could from time to time elevate their mating, and turn it into lovemaking. I vividly remembered the Fairy Maid of the Lake and Aeneas. And I had heard of other humans making love quite unlike animals.

On an island in the midst of my lake, some pious men had founded a monastery. They studied and wrote very many things "for the blessedness of the human race". They were monks, and as such they were supposed to hold in contempt the pleasures of the flesh, I had learned. However, one of them had become involved in an affair with a woman whose beauty was dazzling.

The free-spirited daughter of a local king, there was no wisdom or sobriety in her, only fire and love of life. In the monk, on the other hand, there was genuine spirituality, but also belief in love, and a love not exclusively supreme. The two met, how and why does not matter. They met and met again, always with the cover of darkness.

One summer night they reached me; unrolled a carpet beside my trunk; and made love as if they were possessed. Perhaps they suspected it was their last time together. Never before had I witnessed such insatiable desire.

On their joining together, they seemed not to know what first with hands or eyes they should enjoy, as their passion shifted with trembling unrest. What they grasped, they tightly pressed, as if to seize it. Often their teeth clashed as their mouths struggled together. They sealed each other's mouth with kisses, and they almost hurt each other, turning caresses into stings and vice versa, so that their very bodies no longer knew where and whence to seek mutual pleasure, mutual hurt.

After the blinding heat, love itself appeared to quiet their pains, as if the passionate fire which had set their bodies ablaze could be put out by another fire. That, of course, is unnatural. Fire shall not be extinguished by more fire. And in fact the lovers renewed their lovemaking throughout this inflamed night, locking wildly body onto body, mingling their sweat and the moisture of their mouths, drawing in each other's breath as they pressed madly on their lips, whilst their bodies, mouths, breaths, tried to penetrate one another and merge two souls into one.

Madness? Young lovers' folly? Perhaps, but I cannot forget the words the young princess told the monk, before they departed, at daybreak, never to see each other again.

"Love all that is lovely. Love all you can and *more* than you can."

She was right. When love is to be had, and if it be love and not mere mating, then one should have it, and have it again.

For ages I had favoured certain clouds of pollen that the wind brought to me from far afield. They came from my favourite suitor. All my life I longed to see him, but never could. He grew somewhere windward to me, across the lake, halfway up on a mountain. I always let myself be impregnated by him, and he fathered my dearest offspring. But I was never able to behold him, even less so to caress his leaves and boughs, as the two yews did in my sight.

That is when, I can candidly confess although he is no more, I passionately desired to be... gravitationally unbound. To be on the wing, capable not just of bouncing off the Earth, like a deer on the run, but of leaving it altogether, like a bird taking flight, so as to fly straight to my lover.

I realise that this sounds like a great heresy—a tree which desires to move about like an animal. But I will not recant. There is nothing to recant. Are there not, on this Earth, flightless birds? And mammals that live in the water? Why, I have heard much about dolphins swimming in a bay not far from here, in the expanse of the vast sea. Yet, they milk their young just as women do. So if a bird had wanted to be flightless, if a mammal had wanted to be a fish, and if both had been granted their wish, could I not, at least for once, move so as to be beside my lover? And love him the way young lovers do?

In my miraculously long life, I have mastered many an art, outlived many organisms, come to know things whose existence man does not even suspect. But love's loving embrace, I was not allowed to experience. Young lovers living on this common Earth of ours, take heed: When love comes alive, and if it is astir, then love without restraint as young lovers do, for love dwells in everyone, and the lover is in you.

Love without restraint as young lovers do,
for love dwells in everyone, and the lover is in you.

NINE

One beautiful day in which everything stood still but the sun
walking past his airy ways, Herringbone wended to my
forest. Did I mention that it had been raining for ages? Did I say
that winds and even breezes had forgotten to blow? Did I tell you
about the livelier hue of blue which was dyeing the sky that
summer morning? No, I did not; I'm afraid I have failed to recount
many things. So, let me set Herringbone aside for a while and
update you on the post-war period.

I had prevailed, as you know, but at a price. Namely, my loyal
subjects had lost confidence in me and were fearful of my might,
or should I say brute force? I am certain that was how they called
it among themselves. As a consequence, I was lonely. I found that
I hated solitude as much as I had hated the oaks. So as to defeat
it, I perceived I must wage a quite different war, one of love.

The strawberry tree had fallen prey to an illness. At first I
thought it could deal with it by itself. But it became evident that
my dearest friend was in dire straits. It needed help, its very life
was at stake. I wanted to come to its rescue, and *not* in order to
persuade my woods that I was still a loving queen, but because I
sincerely felt terrible about its suffering.

I did not know what to do, but then I began to wonder if I could
put my growth regulators to use. Not as growth inhibitors, this
time, but as growth *promoters*. Could I help its metabolism by
means of the very substances I sporadically used to help my own?

Within one summer, the strawberry tree revived. Every plant
in the forest knew that its recovery was nothing miraculous, but
rather the outcome of my deliberate efforts.

Little by little, I regained the confidence of the woods. Then I was invaded by what before the war I would have considered not a pretty flower but a rampant weed: a spreading carpet of wood sorrels, beneath me, round my trunk. Because of my embittering experience of loneliness, I welcomed them with open arms, so to speak. In a bid to relate to you, humans, now and then I borrow expressions from your vocabulary which involve parts of your body. But then, does it take a heart to be warm-hearted? The wood sorrels knew it did not. As soon as they understood that I was greeting them defences down, they engulfed me in the softest embrace. At the same time, I had instructed all yews to exude as many growth promoters as possible. They did so enthusiastically. Within a few springs, the forest thrived once more under the just rule of a matriarch of a yew, and under a sky full of rain, sunshine and bliss.

Wasn't this high time to enjoy some of the first-rate entertainment only man could provide with his freakish vagaries?

We had not seen many humans during the last few centuries. Not that I missed their destructive force, about which I had been getting depressing reports from trees all over the land. Alas, my Island had been almost entirely deforested by man and his evil ways—axes, saws, burnings, girdlings. As luck would have it, what I deemed the navel of the universe—my forest—happened to be off the beaten track, in a remote corner of the world. As is often the case, it was just a matter of perspective: the centre of the universe for me was, for man, the periphery.

The sort of human entertainment I longed for presented itself on that breathless summer day I was telling you about, and in the guise of Herringbone.

He did not come stalking across my woods—he stole through them skulkingly. By then I had seen quite a collection of human bipeds, but by the looks of this particular one I knew I was in for something special. He had bristly hair atop and round about his head. That was not the worst, because he was so skinny and hollowed out that, had his head been hairless and his sunken cheeks clean-shaven, he positively would have looked as if he were a wandering skull. Pity his hair could not cover his body entirely, like the boar's bristles, for his clothes were as ragged as a scarecrow's. So decrepit were they, it was remarkable that they had not disintegrated yet. I suspected that, after they had been discarded by beggars as useless cast-offs, he had taken them so as to improve his wardrobe. Lastly, he smelled like fish of the worst sort, by which I mean dead fish that has been out of water, in warm weather, for about four days and four nights. That is one of the reasons why those who bothered to entertain any relationship with him called him Herringbone. Yet, since very few people ever called him anything at all, I should enlist a few more reasons behind his fishy sobriquet.

He loved the taste of fish, and, whenever he could lay his bony hands on a fish—fresh or spoilt he knew no difference—he would clean it most methodically, and then eat it with unspeakable satisfaction. Also, he looked bony, even scaly. And, just like a fish, easy to lure, or, away with euphemisms, downright boneheaded. Yet, he had a prepossessing appearance.

For a creature whose life must be utterly sunless, there was a restoring sunniness about him. Despite his existence forlorn of any comfort, his starved walking skeleton, and the rancid stench which made men and women alike shun him, he felt genuinely happy to be alive and... not particularly well, alas. Why, of course: a man's life is a short one, and shorter still when devoid even of the barest necessities.

If entertainment was what I lacked, I could detect much promise in Herringbone. He needed, however, some directions, which I would attempt to communicate to him.

This was a refreshing idea, to talk to a man. Until then, unlike all other animals and with the noticeable exception of the Green Man, humans had seemed utterly deaf and incapable of dialogue with us. To put my resolve into practice, Herringbone had to remain in my presence long enough. Luckily, it just so happened that on this delightful day a spirited trout leapt towards a fly, overreached, and got stranded on the beach, helpless as any fish out of water. Herringbone sighted it, and turned it forthwith into his supper, breakfast, and—

—"What a fishy lake!" he thought whilst he neatly cleaned his catch. "I wonder if this trout has many brothers and sisters?"

He was about to ask the fish, directly, but realised it was too late, and put the thought past his mind. However, he was confident that he could catch more fish. That he did, in point of fact. So, he took up his lodgings beside me.

One hundred years before the appearance of Herringbone, a rather coarse and hot-tempered king called William Rufus had been killed by an arrow hurled by a crossbow made of yew. And very soon, another hot-tempered but much grander king named Lion Heart would be killed by another arrow from a bow made of yew. Yes, no less than the famous lion-hearted king.

You may be wondering how I could know, back then, what "lion-hearted" meant. Had I ever seen a lion? Of course not! But I had begun to come into contact with a kindred species, that of a tree much akin to us yews, a Podocarpus, which grew in a hot land, under a strong sun, and surrounded by outlandish animals. One of these was their king: a fierce predator resembling a big cat with a mane. Indeed, the lion.

Another Podocarpus species dwelled in a land farther away yet, an immense island which man would discover one day, and consider a continent. Very odd animals roamed there, one of them bouncing off its hind legs and carrying its young inside a pouch on its belly.

Evidently, this connection that I was beginning to experience was far beyond the interconnectedness I had with all trees on my Island via underground fungal filaments. This sort of new and far-reaching communication must be airborne, or something ethereal of that sort.

I know now that it was something better than what present-day humans would call a radio transmission. I was gradually coming into direct contact with species very similar to mine, by picking up their resonance rather than their radio signals, which, of course, they were not broadcasting. But more on this later. Let me go back to the yew bows, and then to Herringbone.

Long before the time of the lion-hearted king, an invading people had defeated the neighbouring island's natives thanks to the formidable weapon they used, the longbow. The invaders occupied the island and developed the weapon, and for hundreds of years thereafter it would be the master of the field and the primary weapon of conquest. Thanks to the yew bow, the neighbouring island rose to the first position among the nations this side of the world. And, by force of such a weapon, it inspired terror and commanded reverence throughout the continental lands. Nevertheless, my Island's people were still largely unacquainted with the use of the bow.

Herringbone, who was having a love affair with the lake's waters for they abounded with fish, had caught a few glimpses of this formidable weapon. Like most beggars, he used to travel from fair to fair in search of alms. At such fairs there were many things to be had and enjoyed, that is, for those who could afford to have and enjoy. Among such things, an archery contest would often be held. Thus Herringbone was introduced to this weapon, so much more lethal than spears. That was all he knew about it. He had never got close to one. On the contrary, when attending a fair, he had always kept slightly farther away than a bow's cast, just in case. But I was looking for some diversion, I had a fine specimen of human quirkiness within reach, and would not waste this marvellous opportunity.

I began to influence him *subliminally*, one may say. Mind you, his was a candid, wholly unassuming soul. I could not have done the same with just any human. Gradually, I succeeded in steering his otherwise highly unengaged attention towards myself, especially my wood, and in making him think about it in connection with those longbows—or bent branches—he had seen in the hands of archers.

In short, he realised that there was one side branch of mine which had the ideal dimensions for a six-foot-tall longbow. That branch he snatched off me. Well, he did not quite snatch it off, but use a saw he did. Since he used his fish knife—the only tool he possessed—you can imagine why such a simple operation took him all summer. Then, unhindered by the cold of winter, he proceeded to make it into a bow.

When I woke next spring I found that he had come up with a fine weapon: a wide-limbed flat bow, with my sapwood as its back, my heartwood as its belly. The arrows he had made out of birch wood, and as for the string's hemp, that I did not know where he had found it. Had he become a skilled bowman? I could not answer the question, for I noticed that instead of hunting, as every respectable bowman would do when not at war, he fished. Only, with bow and arrows, and with such poor results that in time he resolved, albeit reluctantly, to leave my forest in pursuit of his favourite food—fish.

But as he roamed far and wide, he came to the conclusion that he was neither fisherman nor huntsman. In spite of his newly acquired weapon, which, I must report, he used more as an oversized staff than as a bow, he knew full well what he was. A beggar at heart, with no banquet, or meal of any sort, to attend.

One day, as he sat idly along a highway waiting for nothing in particular, his life came to a turning point.

A horse-driven carriage emerged from the mist and solemnly drew near him.

"This must be the carriage of a great lord," he thought; "great riches must be riding in it." Then, as any half-starved beggar would have hoped, he added: "Let there be a kind-hearted man in it."

In Herringbone's life many invocations had gone unheard, many people had turned their head the other way when he had stretched his begging hand. Some of these, the haughty ones, had kicked him or had him thrown into the mud by heartless thugs. So, what else was new? The man riding in the carriage would probably pay no attention to a filthy beggar, and the carriage's wheels would splash muddy water over his bony body. But there *was* something new. Beside him, there lay that wooden branch he had carved off me. And it was not merely a shapely piece of durable wood, not merely a powerful weapon. It was a part of Me, I, the Queen of the Forest and of the Island—one not to be trifled with, one not likely to suffer an affront.

Yet, this hapless beggar hardly ever used my bow. I was beginning to feel I had been let down, for I was not being entertained, but only indirectly humbled. And that I could not bear.

He had come up with a fine weapon: a wide-limbed flat bow,
with my sapwood as its back, my hardwood as its belly.

As the carriage drew closer, and closer still, Herringbone stood up and instead of stretching out his trembling hand, he put forth his deadly longbow. Next, with a new sound in his voice, and more air from his lungs, he said: "Your money or your life!"

The coachman stopped the carriage, and a man's head leant out from the side, saying: "Did I hear you right?"

"Your money or your life, I said."

The man's head looked as if it belonged to a grand and proud person. He answered: "What do you mean, you scummy leech? Do you mean to threaten me with your bow?"

"Indeed I do."

"Then," he retorted coolly, "you should like to know that your bow is unstrung."

As Herringbone remembered that he had taken the string off it a few days before—or was it a few weeks?—the grand and proud man became grander and prouder, whereas he shrank back into his lifelong inconspicuousness.

"Oh dear," said Herringbone, terror-stricken, "oh dear. Your Worship, you see, I am no highwayman, of course. Just a... bowman."

"But of course. A bowman holding an unstrung bow with which he threatens me."

"Not at all, your Worship! Pray let me explain. I meant to warn your Worship, for I've heard of a fearsome highwayman who robs worthy Lords by saying 'Your money or your life.'"

"Then yours was but a friendly warning?"

"So it was, your Worship."

Well, the grand and proud man was not travelling alone, but escorted by some thugs. They gave Herringbone a good thrashing and then, at his Worship's behest, stripped him of his tattered rags and tossed him into a puddle. Such a puddle was not shallow but deep enough for him to drown in, since, always at his Worship's behest, his head was pressed hard against the bottom for quite some time. If the water did not choke him, it was only thanks to his name and fishlike inclinations.

Herringbone sorely learnt his lesson. The next time he held up a carriage, his bow was strung, drawn, and ready to fling an arrow. He hurt no-one, for he loathed bloodshed, but got his money and took to the woods. Not just any woods. By way of untrodden paths, he came back to pay me tribute in his awkward but heartfelt fashion.

On the way to my forest, he had to cross a highway and, as chance would have it, stumbled upon the same grand and proud man to whom he said: "Your money or your life!"

"Well, well, well, look who's here. How did you like your bath? Did it deliver you from your filth?"

"Your money or your life, I said!"

"I heard you, my jolly leech, I heard you. Do tell me: how do you mean to persuade me to give up my money, this time? You are not even holding your bow."

"You do not want to have me hold my bow."

"But I do, I do! I'd love to behold your extraordinary imbecility once more. It'll help my digestion. And then I'll enjoy myself even more when I see you beaten to death. I say: show your petty bow, you scummy leech!"

"If that is your wish—"

—With unexpected swiftness, he reached to the ground, grabbed the longbow, drew it, and shot an arrow that flew straight to, and *through*, the man's nose.

As blood gushed out of His Worship's face, the thugs took to their heels. The beggar shouted: "Tell the people this was the work of Herringbone!"

When he came back to me I told him, not directly, but I made myself understood, that he had graduated to the rank of active beggar. Though he would still have to wait for almsgivers, he had a more persuasive way of obtaining his alms. Then I suggested he get himself a new set of clothes, real clothes, not rags; a horse; and a meal or two a day. Above all, I put a flea in his ear (which felt immediately at home) as a reminder of the following. "Wander off and catch up on all the living you've missed; most of all, make the best of it."

Although I did not mention anything about keeping clean, one afternoon he moved his steps towards the lake with the apparent intention of bathing in it. I half panicked, for I feared his putrid stench might kill the fish and poison the roots of lakeside plants, among them the strawberry tree. But a providential lightning grazed him, and the ensuing rainstorm showered him to his satisfaction.

Off he went. Through my bough, which he had turned into his weapon of emancipation, I thought I'd be a witness of many highway robberies and narrow escapes. I was in for some surprises.

Regular fishy meals, new clothes, baths and showers here and there revived his weary body, and let his innate sunniness shine forth. Herringbone gradually metamorphosed into a handsome and gallant man, always heading sunwards, even under the not infrequent deluges that came scudding in from the ocean.

"I owe it all to a stick, a wooden stick. I can't believe it," he would often repeat. So he took a liking to trees, flowers, birds and sun-loving things. Which, rest assured, included the fair sex.

Until his metamorphosis, he had only fancied women, who had remained a mystery to him. It must be owned that there was little appeal in his ragged looks and rancid stench. His robberies brought him silver, far more silver than he needed, for he remained surprisingly frugal. One day, as he galloped off from one of his robberies, he sighted a lovely girl milking a cow. He approached her and, sitting astride his black steed, said: "Fair maiden of the meadow, your bowman pure in heart is thirsty and would like to quench his thirst."

"Is that so? And how would you like to go about it?"

"If that would please you, I'd like to dismount from my horse and drink something in your company."

"I have fresh milk or plain water."

"Milk will be fine."

"It will cost you."

"I shall pay in advance, my fair maiden. There, take this. Is it enough for a bucketful of milk?"

The milkmaid picked up the pouch he had thrown at her graceful feet and, as she counted the silver pieces it contained, could not believe her luck.

"Your Worship, you can buy the whole cow with this, even a herd of cattle. Your Worship, where are you?"

He turned up behind her, gave her a bunch of wildflowers he had just gathered, and whispered: "Some milk will do. And don't you ever Worship me."

A kiss ensued, quickly chased by another one. They were both novices, and it took them a few days of loving practice to understand the game of give and take. These could not have been sunnier days.

He continued to go to fairs, but with a different perspective. There were tuneful minstrels to listen to, and complaisant damsels with whom to exchange compliments. He discovered that he cherished mirth and merriment, only, what mirth had there ever been in his life before the longbow? None whatsoever: fighting with a fellow beggar over a tattered blanket; or wrestling with his gut over hunger pangs, and the food that was amiss and that had always been more than scarce. And at the fairs, as well as by the wayside, there were always the beggars, the sick, the forsaken. But he had not forgotten his hardships. He would arrive at a fair rich in silver; leave it rich in gratefulness. He never turned his head the other way when he encountered a needy wretch. Most of what he took, he gave away, and only thus, he believed, did life make sense.

Was he an outlaw? The people he robbed, what laws did they abide by? Weren't their laws ones of confiscation and plunder? Laws such as he did know—but still feared—he didn't like, for it seemed to him that lawmakers were themselves bandits, only greedier by far.

At a fair he came across a buffoon who managed to identify him regardless of his disguise. He did not divulge his discovery, but composed a little poem in Herringbone's honour.

> Stealing money, jewels or wealth
> Is no crime
> As long as it is done with stealth.

But I am not here to sanctify anyone, let alone a lowly biped. I wish, however, to relate what I saw through my branch-turned-longbow. Such as many robberies, to be sure. But also many deeds of gallantry, and many heartfelt expressions of generosity.

Lawfully wedded wives of grand and proud men secretly hoped to meet him and steal a shred of his sunniness; to lie in his arms in a wide-open field over a carpet of wildflowers. Some of them got what they coveted. His archery skills improved as more and more sheriffs tried to hunt him down. Likewise, his loving abilities were perfected as more and more women came to prize his kisses far above gold.

A handful of sheriffs and their thugs were determined to put an end to his banditry. One rainy night he fell prey to an ambush. He shot but one arrow, and that to the stars.

Everyone across my Island thought he had died there, but *I* can tell you it was not so. Somehow, he had managed to escape, carrying his sunniness and his bow away with him.

After living on the dodge for a few seasons, he travelled across a great wide channel, and landed on the neighbouring island, towards the rising sun. There, under a new name many of you are familiar with, he turned his feats into an enterprise of redistribution, which involved many merry bowmen. His chivalrous deeds were celebrated in ballads, poems, and legends. Someday, they will become myths.

Such lore, however, the kind listener will have to seek elsewhere. Due to the greater distance from me in both space and time, the signals I received from Herringbone's bow began to blur, until they faded altogether.

TEN

In you, my kind human listeners, ageing begins as soon as adulthood is reached. Since you are fond of life, you wish you could be forever young. Yet, in the entire animal kingdom, maturity forebodes a decrease of several biological functions and, consequently, decline.

On the other hand, among higher plants and particularly among us yews, maturity is a term of more than ordinary vagueness. If judged by the time our crown of branches and leaves starts to decrease in size, maturity can be often around two thousand years. However, if ability to sprout be taken as a sign of immaturity, then even a two thousand-year-old yew must be considered immature, for it can continue to sprout even from the trunk and, in some instances, almost at ground level.

Unlike you, we sustain growth throughout life and, in this sense, we can reasonably claim to be perpetually embryonic. We can be as nearly immortal as any living thing on this planet. So, when I talk about my coming of age, I attach to it a very different meaning.

Do you remember my very early growth, my first enchanting years amid what looked like the garden of earthly delights? When I felt lost, dwarfed by towering trees, I turned to my built-in memory to obtain answers to my searching questions. The answers were not reassuring, but puzzling. I know now that my memory had not come into focus yet. Intuitively, I addressed my queries to my two mothers, my natural mother, and Mother Nature. But, as I was approaching my fifteen hundredth birthday, my mother had been gone for centuries, and Mother Nature had long stopped sending her go-betweens. Did this imply that my learning process had ended and any new knowledge was to be acquired solely through my experiences? On the contrary, it meant that, as I had finally come of age, my built-in memory had come into focus.

The first signs of such new powers consisted in being able to arrive at different, distant places without travelling, as I have mentioned in passing. First, through the kindred Podocarpus tree. Then, through other conifers, such as pines, firs, cypresses and so forth.

One of these species was particularly impressive: the Sequoia. I remember how awe-struck I was by the sheer size of this giant. I also recall, however, finding this display of height, volume, girth—and I could go on and on about its massive attributes—rather ostentatious. In any case, it was against my principle, which preaches that if one wants to live a long life, one had better keep a low profile.

After the conifers, I began to see also through broad-leafed trees, such as oaks, beeches, maples... These were stunning faculties. I was coming into direct contact with thousands and thousands of species previously wholly unknown to me, from all corners of the Earth, and millions and millions of individual plants.

How could that be? How could I roam through space so effortlessly? Actually, quite simply. As you know, it had all started with the Podocarpus, a species very akin to us yews. Then it had moved on to the next in the line of botanical proximity, as it were. And then on to the next, until it had reached very odd plants, such as palms, cacti, mangroves.

Having become able to spill over into other plants' fields of form, I had gradually "branched out", quite fittingly. Every species has a field of form, and mine being very similar to that of the Podocarpus, it made sense that I pervaded that particular one first. And then on to the next, one by one, until I was interconnected with all species on Earth.

Let it be understood that I was being privileged. Only trees of great age and great... knowledge can invade amicably the fields of form of other trees. As for you humans, I will not say that it is impossible and beyond your powers. If I do not rule out the possibility it is because something of the kind has happened, and I have witnessed it. You have guessed whom I am referring to, haven't you? The Green Man. That memorable day in which he ate my berries and drank the tea he had brewed with my leaves, he, a man, rather than dying of this poison potion, became capable of hearing me. He had spilled over into *my* field of form, which to this date remains an almost miraculous occurrence, for a man's field of form, as you can imagine, is utterly unlike a tree's.

Roaming freely through space and getting to see exotic places, plants, and animals entertained me for a few years of otherwise peaceful existence. But the wonderful surprises were far from over. Any individual is embedded into its surroundings, whereas I, for whichever generous concession, was granted the extraordinary possibility to roam not only in space, but also in time.

This is what I mean by coming of age.

Most lowly species—man included—may occasionally feel a blurred, indistinct echo coming from the past. These are flashes, inexplicable *déjà vu*. If the most perceptive among you can see a few fleeting flashes of mysterious things past, *I* saw the entire layout of history and prehistory, receding almost three hundred million years back in time! As this colossal amount of information was all accurately laid down before me, I was introduced to the immense ebb and flow of the past since the advent of the first yew on Earth. Even for me, the indomitable Queen of the Forest, it was overwhelming.

Eventually, I reconciled myself to the fact that it made sense that only I, and a few more members of this very exclusive club, could have access to such a stupendous memory. It would have been wasted on a rose, a birch, or even an oak—too short-lived, what could they do with all this information? Not enough time to let it seep through and sink in.

I soon recognised how foolish I had been to feel proud about my venerable age, which had been attained, no doubt, also at the expense of other species, as the oaks had experienced on their own... bark. My 1430 springs, although monumental when compared to the life span of a lesser tree, were as nothing next to the history of the yew tree since its inception, and still nothing next to the concept of Time on a geological scale.

My stupendous memory would allow me to make what is generally defined "time immemorial" to become "memorial"—this time out of mind, beyond memory or record, which was about to resurface and unveil its secrets to me.

With devouring curiosity, I plunged into time travel, starting from the very beginning, the first appearance of the yew family founder on Earth. I reached back years, decades, centuries, millennia, tens and hundreds of thousands of years, till the dizzying speed of my journey back in time started to diminish. Then I was overpowered by a bizarre and most unlikely sensation, particularly for a tree. I felt as if I were... flying, gliding smoothly over unknown lands. I could distinguish no separate large islands, the different continents that make up the world as we know it. From the giddy heights of my flight I could behold one continuous land mass, towards which I began a slow descent. As, with unspeakable relief, I found myself once again rooted in the ground, I immediately gazed out on every side.

In the mist of a warm swamp, among other odd leafy stumps, I could see a magnificent specimen of a tree which closely resembled us yews. My memory promptly informed me that it was what present-day scientists have unearthed as fossils and indicated as the founder of my genus, the prototype of all yews.

She, for it was a female, did not differ dramatically from me; just slightly more savage, but seemingly already capable of great longevity, as I was told that she was several centuries old. Some time after her coming into being, the first male yew came along too, and reproduction thus commenced.

This was our primeval beginning as well as the beginning of my investigations, which I conducted incessantly, rain or shine, for years, trying to be, as ever, the first tree to wake and the last one to fall asleep.

My reign did not suffer from lack of leadership for, at long last, my offspring were in sight. They had reached me. The individual tree does not move, but the *community* tree does.

The community tree is the group of trees of the same

species—in this instance, the yews I had mothered—connected by root grafts. My offspring's community had been constantly on the move, as new parts of it, new yew trees, had grown into new spatial positions. After the massacre of the oaks, they had found no major obstacle in making their way towards me. By the time I was finally able to see them, they had grown into a thick woodland at the expense of other species, which they had pushed to the forest's edges. I could now appoint one of my offspring as temporary ruler of the forest and travel back in time for as long as I deemed it necessary. A motherly listener may object:

"Why did you choose to abstract yourself from your surroundings after having waited so long to see your sons and daughters? Now that you finally could, why neglect them?"

What can I say? I see what you mean, and can even admit that you are right, especially in view of what was to happen to me shortly after this period. But my memory enabled me only to remember, not to remember *forwards*. I could not foresee the future, still cannot, and... I had to make a choice between the company of my offspring and that of history and prehistory. Perhaps I was a matriarch more than a mother. Perhaps one simply can't have it all.

To return to my time travel. Having over two hundred million years at one's disposal is a more than intoxicating prospect. Like the restless young lovers I told you about, the princess and the monk, I too did not know what first to enjoy. But I soon realised that in the whole of prehistory there was no better show, no more exhilarating entertainment, than the one provided by the dinosaurs. If you think a fish is dim-witted and a shrimp even worse, let me acquaint you with the dinosaurs I had the chance to watch in action.

The world today is so full of people and rats, bugs, and what not, it seems unearthly to think that once, some time after the advent of yews on Earth, giant lizards had the whole planet to themselves. What use did they make of it?

I soon discovered that their feeble intellect was probably but "Phase I" of the thinking machine Mother Nature was trying to assemble and install into the skulls of animals. Dinosaurs thought clumsily and moved about just as clumsily.

At first, they fed on one another to such an extent that they

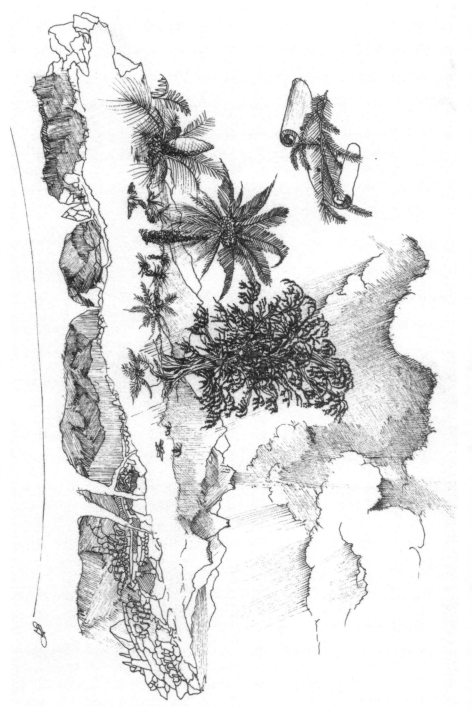

I reached back years, decades, centuries, millennia, tens and hundreds of thousands of years.

kept flirting with self-inflicted extinction. Good grief, they were always hungry and made no distinction between their kin and other species. I saw mothers eat their young, and brothers chew on one another. It was sickening, yet fun. At least I could experience gluttony and avidity first hand, and keep it in mind in terms of what animals—and man specifically—have done to the world since.

In time, some dinosaurs turned to leaves, grasses, and seaweed for food. This too proved to be quite a spectacle. They started to graze on leaves, so that they would not have to bend their long necks. At times, one would slowly and deliberately chew up all the leaves of a yew, only to discover, later on, when nothing could be done about it, that they were poisonous. So they would lie on the ground helplessly, and form a cavity in it, because they weighed an absurdity. Invariably, they died in excruciating agony, and usually burst open, since a heart attack in those huge beasts implied a small earthquake. Their guts and bowels were scattered by their devastating explosions till the landscape became gracefully dotted with their tripe. Nor did their descendants learn from experience.

In the millions of years dinosaurs stumbled across the Earth, they continued to eat yew leaves and die because of them. However, when they grazed on something harmless, not knowing moderation, they overgrazed. Then, they unfailingly fell prey to most debilitating cases of diarrhœa, truly monstrous, both in size and rankness. The flesh-eating dinosaurs, on the other hand, had been fitted with a poorly functioning gut which, more often than not, forced them to vomit their meals.

In other words, wasn't the world an idyllic place? Ah, the good old days... Here beckoned a Brontosaurus, so heavy that it could hardly walk, spending most of its time in the water, that was, *if* it mastered the sophisticated art of staying afloat (half of them drowned). And there came wobbling a fierce Tyrannosaurus Rex, King of the Dinosaurs, its long tail trying, but not always managing, to counterbalance its body; its forelimbs dangling limp and useless; its sharp teeth often sinking by mistake into its own tongue. And the heavenly scenery, cheerfully sprinkled with their fæces, vomit, exploded or half-eaten corpses slowly rotting away...

Modern-day palæontologists are baffled by the disappearance of the dinosaurs. They ought to be saddened by it too. Such crotchety creatures deserved to live on. You may ask:

"Since you claim to know it all, tell us: whatever happened to the dinosaurs? Did they really become extinct, and if so, why? Or did they evolve into other animals?"

Have you mistaken me for an encyclopædia? Even if my knowledge is far vaster than what you appreciate as encyclopædic, it does not mean that I care to answer. Besides, sooner or later you will come up with the right answer. Just bear in mind that dinosaurs were so clumsy that they crushed more than half the eggs they sat on...

You see, Mother Nature was then younger too, and not exactly infallible. It is a fact that she had already engineered truly accomplished marvels, such as the yew tree, but you should consider us beginner's luck. For the most part, she used to make resounding mistakes. She is still working on the "eternal fitness of things", and I'm beginning to wonder if she will ever bring off her ambitious goal?

But, as the dinosaurs left the stage, in came the early mammals, and then the infamous newcomer—man.

Mankind is a relatively recent pest, for the entire duration of humankind on Earth is like the flapping of a butterfly's wings when compared to the span of us yews. Notwithstanding that, mankind has gone a long way from its faltering beginnings.

The oldest known wooden tool, a 50,000-year-old spear, was recently unearthed by present-day archaeologists. Wouldn't you know it, it is made of yew. Man eventually discovered how hard and resilient our wood was, and began to use it for his tools and weapons. Still, it must be acknowledged that it took some bravery to kill a straight-tusked elephant by means of a few pointed sticks. That is why we began to be harvested.

I find that my ancestors did not particularly mind that. Man looked like one more of Mother Nature's experiments. However, it soon became clear that, unlike dinosaurs, man was perfectible through the sorry process of trial and error.

I saw primitive men learn to walk on two legs only. Saw their arms gradually shrink and their jaws and teeth become smaller.

Saw them, terrified as night fell, run for cover, and sleep wrapped in leaves and leafy branches. Then they stopped bawling at the stars to invoke the return of the sun, because they understood that the sun would return anyway, and quite regularly. Often they surrendered their caves to wild animals, and often lay hopeless on the ground after having being torn by the merciless jaws of savage beasts. Others were spared thanks to hasty retreats, but, wounded, they clasped their trembling hands over their bleeding wounds, and wailed and howled into the dead of night till death delivered them from such a torture, helpless as they were and unaware of any cure.

Meanwhile, we yews stood our ground. When my predecessors were already waging victorious chemical wars that made them one of the co-dominant species of trees on Earth, men were cracking each other's skulls with wooden clubs.

Eventually, they began to understand more about life and its cycles, and emancipated themselves through us plants. Agriculture made them forever different from all other animals.

I learnt that man's coming of age brought about our decline. Not that we were in any way weaker, or less long-lived. We were relentlessly preyed upon. From the dawning of Western Civilisation all through Herringbone's time, great armies were fitted out by us yews. We were felled by the thousands, by the tens, hundreds of thousands.

I should state that neither in my many travels back in time, nor in my direct experiences, have I ever seen a human female— a woman—fell a yew. Nor have I seen women kill their kin or act with gratuitous cruelty. Even though there have been exceptions, what I am about to say is not the exception, but the rule. Women have always been responsible for procreation; men have made themselves recurrently known for their appetite for destruction. Human history reads like a long litany of aggressions, lootings, and burnings in which women seldom took part, but in which they were often victimised. Men coveted us yews for our wood, which they would turn into bows, weapons of conquest; women prized flowers for their forms, colours, and fragrances. It was women who went, and go, through the pangs of labour and delivery, not men. Every woman knows how hard and painful it is to create. Man knows how easy it is to destroy. If there is hope for the Earth, then it rests on women's shoulders.

I must at this point pass from prehistory to history, and then to my chronicle.

A few years after I had come of age, a local chieftain, with old age advancing, sought to amend his ways by building an abbey. Attracted by heavenly music (which I never heard), he came upon my woods, precisely where I had been standing for 1446 years, and thereon ordered the building of an abbey.

This was great news. The custom of the churchyard yew had grown out of earlier religious beliefs and man had finally come up with a way of protecting us. Every church was endowed with one yew tree, and at times two, within its grounds. We represented immortality and kept vigil on man's dead relations and friends. Albeit somewhat dispiriting, this implied being out of the clutches of military man, with his thirst for bows. And now an abbey would be built beside me. It entailed ensured survival. I probably had been chosen for my inspiring size and venerable age to be a link between past and present.

Upon hearing about this novel human enterprise, I resumed the leadership of the forest, and temporarily put aside my stupendous memory and the diversions it afforded, so as to get ready for more entertainment—men at work. Reluctantly, I went to sleep, looking forward to reawakening towards the end of winter.

ELEVEN

During the warmer months of the 1446th year since my birth, my leaves ran their course. After six years of dedicated work they turned brown, ready to be shed. Which I did, bidding them a grateful farewell.

I wanted to display myself at my best, delighted at the idea that monarchs and dignitaries of the church would come to visit the abbey which was to be built. I hurried into the production of a fresh crop of leaves.

By the end of spring I looked splendid. My sheer size, first of all, was sensational. Although a yew's chief objective in life is not to attain great size but great age, centuries of vigorous growth had contributed to my monumental dimensions. It would have taken eight women or six men to embrace my trunk. The latter had been hollow for a few centuries, but that did not prevent me from thriving. The heartwood at my trunk's centre would gradually die off, and I would "shed" (with the help of some harmless fungi which fed only on dead wood) that part of me which had become functionless. It may be argued that, albeit dead, this inner wood could give me strength and support. That, however, was hardly my case. Not having to contend with a great height, I was not apt to blow over. What mattered was the sapwood beneath my bark. Functions essential to my well-being occurred there, and, I can joyfully report, continued to occur smoothly, almost effortlessly, as if driven by the great inertia of centuries of practice.

Was there a lovelier sight than the exquisite purple-brown of my bark? The pale green of my new crop of leaves? Well, yes, perhaps there was a lovelier sight still: that of the aforementioned hues with the bright red of my berries sprinkled amid them. That would happen in a few moons, as, early every autumn, I punctually came into fruit.

My roots had long since mastered the art of rock-splitting. I would have them burrow into the cracks and crevices of the limestone I grew upon, and then would feel them swell and expand in girth. The force thus exerted was such that it resulted in widening the cracks between the rocks and actually splitting them apart.

All the yews in the forest revered me not only as their ruler—and, in many cases, as their mother—but also as an emblem. They regarded me as living proof of how a wilful yew could and would implement all her powers so as to mitigate the elements and nullify her few enemies. In fact, I was a source of inspiration for all trees on the Island, and my war tactics were being analysed by many a leading tree aspiring to gain unchallenged leadership within its forest.

That flattered me, and did not worry me. No matter how thorough a study these trees might conduct, it still took a yew, and quite a remarkable one, to carry out successfully the chemical warfare I had pioneered on my Island.

So I reigned over my verdant woods, as justly as natural laws would allow. As ever, I cherished the bountiful rain, the lively air, the playful sun, the peaceful moon and distant stars. I had had the good fortune of living a wonderful life. True, I would have preferred not to have been compelled to wage a war. Even truer, I had some regrets, the most tormenting of which was not to have understood that my mother was dying. But I had been giving that period of my life much thought, lately, and had come to the conclusion that I had the right to question her white lies. What had she accomplished by her prevarication? By pretending to be all right when in truth she was in agony? Had she spared me from sorrow? On the contrary.

Notwithstanding the respect and, above all, the love I felt for her, I had grown critical of her conduct. Had she been shrewder and sterner, she could have had a longer life. That would have prevented the loss of the status quo in the forest, which encouraged the oaks to revolt against a crumbling hierarchy, and which, ultimately, forced me to engage in a long and devastating conflict.

I was persuaded that I had already achieved better and more resounding results than she had. The mere fact that I, unlike her, had been given full access to the stupendous built-in memory attested to the soundness of my achievements. Perhaps I could not be as motherly and sweet, but sweetness, I'm afraid, is a luxury one had better forgo when in power.

Adorned by new leaves, and atwitter with goldcrests, robins, blue tits and chaffinches amid my mighty branches, I eagerly awaited the humans in charge of building the abbey. I did not have to wait long.

Despite a drenching rainy day, a dozen friars arrived at the building site. They brought along oxen whose duty consisted in pulling carts on which were amassed the building materials and the tools needed for the construction.

This slow procession went on for days, indeed for weeks. There was something quite solemn about it, perhaps appropriately so, since they were to build not just any dwelling, but a place of worship. By eavesdropping on the monks' conversations, I gradually learnt that they belonged to a mendicant order founded by a holy man in a distant land. He had been canonised owing to his compassionate conduct, which had become famous because, among other things, it included talking to animals and plants.

"I couldn't have been luckier," I thought. "This site was certainly selected for its natural beauty, which must have inspired these kindly men."

I remember that, whilst I was blessing my good fortune for having brought to me these sedulous men, the holly tree warned me: "Man is never to be trusted. No matter how meek he seems, he is *always* treacherous."

She had grown older and lost some of her attractiveness. That was all I could notice. Did I pay attention to her warning? Of course not. If centuries ago I had thought her half-witted, she must have got even worse in the meantime.

Having piled up an impressive amount of materials, the friars were ready to start the construction by digging trenches along the perimeter of the abbey-to-be, wherein to lay the foundations. During a morning in which rain and shine were strangely mixed, I saw the men of the cloth pick up their digging tools and direct their steps towards me.

But what tools were those which they held in their hands? Were they picks and shovels they brandished as they drew near? Where was the pointed head of their picks? Why was it a bladed head? And that long, toothed blade, what was that? It was not a shovel, it couldn't be. And why had they got so close to me? Surely with all the space available they couldn't intend to raise one of the abbey's walls immediately next to me. And why was it that they had not drawn, on the ground, the perimeter of the building? Were they going to dig the trenches without following a precise layout? It would be unlike them—they had so neatly divided and piled up all the building materials, and kept track of them in writing... They couldn't suddenly change and act so slovenly...

Then came the first blow. It landed on the mossy, northern side of my trunk, "The Devil's side," I heard them say.

"Let us start here for an auspicious beginning. Praise the Lord!" and the second blow came crashing down, followed by another one, chased ever so quickly by more and more blows.

What were they doing, these crazed beasts? Was this the duty of a man of the cloth, a man of the cross, that wooden cross they all bowed to—to turn into an axeman? Lowly, vile, predatory beasts: What were they, what were they doing to me? Why? How dare they? What sacrilegious hand dared violate Me, the Queen of the Forest? How could they drive the iron blades of their axes, the sharp teeth of their saws into me?

The pain, the Pain was tearing me apart. For a moment I thought I could endure, I could bear it. I tried to pretend it wasn't happening, and perhaps it was not, perhaps it was a nightmare. I had never had nightmares, but wasn't this a strange day, one of rain and shine mixed together? It was a nightmare of pain, pain so intoxicating that, at length, it seemed sweet.

When the blows came in an uninterrupted succession, it felt as if I were being uprooted, thrown up in the air by a force insane, subjected to something so unnatural that it could make me do things extraordinary. When the axe work stopped, however briefly, the pain caught up to me, the open wounds called me back to this world. Then the sacrilege started again, as the beasts resumed their ungodly hewing. They cut me, slashed me, violated my gentle sapwood, sweeping down, chopping blindly through me and my cells, slaughtering them by the tens of thousands, hundreds of thousands, by the millions... Every blow crashing down cried DIE, DIE, DIE...

I became delirious and saw wolves eating their tails, birds poking holes into the rocky ground, fish running backwards on their fins whilst stags pranced on their hind legs with spider webs on their antlers, every precious animal and plant underneath the stars running, swimming, flying, collapsing to the ground, whilst that which must be the humans' Devil was wedded in the sky and his imps began to throw strange fruits that plummeted viciously like hail, bursting, exploding, staining me deeply red...

I reached a peak of unbearable pain, and finally the featureless darkness of the aftermath.

(The narrative continued by a loyal subject, the juniper.)

Her Majesty the Queen asked me to pick up the story where She left off for a few reasons. First, the fact that, having been felled, she has no recollection of that period of Her life. Second, because even if She did, She would rather refrain from speaking about it. Third, She does not wish to foster the controversy on such an incendiary subject, and that is, the chequered relationship between trees and man.

Although I was not yet alive when our Queen was mercilessly toppled, my mother was. You might remember her as an important member of the Evergreen Club. Shortly before passing away, she told me what had happened to the Queen. As I listened heedfully to her last words, I was chosen as the one who, in turn, would tell you about that stormy period.

What our Queen had interpreted, perhaps a little vainly, as the loveliest sight in the forest—"the exquisite purple-brown of my bark"; "the uncharacteristically pale green of my new crop of leaves"; etc.,—had been utterly misinterpreted by the friars.

The cavernous hollowness of Her trunk and the "ghostly"—so they defined them—purplish bark and pale leaves all conjured up, in their minds, visions of ghosts and things supernatural. The northern part of Her trunk was carpeted with green moss. This, they thought, meant that the part of Her which was oriented to the North—the "sinister Devil's side"—thrived more than any other part. Moreover, the light green of Her leaves was mistaken for a generalised sickly condition, since all the yews they had seen had dark green leaves. Her monumental size was considered unsafe, indeed menacing because of the hollow trunk which "could not possibly support the tree in case of a gale." She did grow in a spot which provided a commanding view, and She was the only... obstacle to the abbey's otherwise unobstructed view of the lake and the mountains. Thus ensued the decision to fell Her and build the abbey above Her roots.

It was a decision made quickly, almost rashly, the night before that mournful day, as barrels of long-awaited red wine had arrived from a southern land. It was intended to be sipped judiciously whilst officiating at mass, where it symbolised the blood of their Saviour. It went down their throats, that night, like a swollen river gurgling impetuously past bridges on its way to the sea.

The next morning, two things remained of their debauched night: a persistent headache, and the resolve to cut down the tree.

Our Queen passed out after a few excruciating hours, but it took the friars months of devoted, if malicious, work to bring Her down to the ground.

What a sorry sight that was! The Proud and Indomitable Queen of the Forest lying prostrate on the rocky ground, reduced to helplessness, cut off from her roots, torn away from life. When she finally collapsed, the friars celebrated the completion of their preliminary clearance for days and nights. Then they chopped

Her up into thousands of little logs so as to have an enormous supply of firewood for the winter.

It was the 1448th year of their Lord. The building of the abbey commenced then.

We trees of the forest felt bereaved. And forsaken, terrified, powerless.

The friars' second illustrious victim was the graceful and age-old Strawberry Tree. It took them far less time to dispose of it, as it was precariously perched on a cliff by the lakeside. They loosened the soil round it, slashed deeply into its roots, and then pushed and pulled, both they and the oxen they had yoked to the task, until the uprooted tree fell into the lake. Then the friars laid out a broad esplanade between the abbey and the lake and, because of this landscaping whim, thus died our Queen's bosom friend.

The story of our Yewess could have ground to a definitive halt at this point. Few trees in the woods nurtured any hope of ever again being ruled and guided by a great Queen. Man was upon us, and he was evil.

(The narrative resumed by me, the Queen of the Forest.)

So it was all over. The leaves fluttering in the breeze, the twigs, branches and limbs that sustained them, the birds that nested on them, the wood mice, badgers, and foxes that had used my hollow trunk as their dwelling. The sky, the rain, the sun, photosynthesis—farewell to life. No more leaves, no more chlorophyll, no more energy absorption, no more food being manufactured. In one word: death.

And yet, something was keeping me alive.

I had lost all of my aboveground self, but underground I had been left untouched. There was food stored there. A good volume in the butt, root-swell and interior lengths of my massive roots. At first, I could have lived on the energy obtainable from these storage cells. I had previously not been aware of this survival tactic. Still, sooner or later, such provisions would run out. Though it might take years to exhaust them, given the monumental volume of my roots, eventually I would be faced with starvation, and death would follow. The survival tactic therefore appeared to be incomplete. As it transpired, it was effective if coupled with another expedient.

Yews sprout readily both from the base and along the stem. As a part of this enthusiastic profusion of life, they also produce epicormic buds. These arise like other side buds, but unlike the usual ones, they do not proceed to extend their leaf or shoot. Their tip grows just enough to remain inside the bark. Each year they lengthen only enough to stay within the bark. Should the stem, by which I also mean the trunk, be broken, these hidden buds, triggered by the sudden failure of the growth regulator that suppresses them—so as to maintain the dominance of the main shoot—burst out, and send forth several shoots.

I had observed something akin to this with my mother, although her trunk had been only partially reduced by a windstorm, never entirely removed like mine. Now that my crown of branches and trunk had been brutally felled, many buds around my base were ready to shoot, powered by the starches in the storage cells.

It did not happen overnight. They had toppled me in April. I regained consciousness by midsummer, and at first I wished I had not. I felt like a fish out of water gasping desperately; like a mole stuck in a burrow after a landslide; like a man trapped in a collapsed mine, scraping and rasping helplessly in the dark as the air becomes unbreathable. But I soon realised that there was a way back to the water; a way around the landslide; a way out of the mine. The pain slowly ceased and the buds readied themselves to issue forth. My command was needed to start life anew. It was not "merely" regeneration, not "merely" a matter of restoring injured and infected cells to their same spatial positions. To arise from my ruins, I had to generate new cells, in a new position. Although endowed with a meandering network of roots, the result of almost fifteen centuries of growth, I still would start out as a dwarf, or a group of dwarfs, that is, a few sprouts. The friars, noticing my minute wobbling stem, or stems, would easily cut me down again. The same procedure would be repeated until I starved to death. Perhaps sooner, as the monks would lay the floor on top of my roots.

My chances of survival were slim. Moreover, to be cut down once was enough. The idea of having my tiny sprouts carelessly yanked by the same evil hands was an additional humiliation—and torture. Many other yews, in the same situation, would have given up and died with dignity. *But*, something stronger than my will wanted to trigger the onset of my life anew. Do you know what it was? Can you imagine what force could be so powerful as to overrule my deliberate decision?

It was hate, my friends, hate. A hate supreme.

Towards the end of summer, as it was getting nippy, the friars began to warm their nights by gathering round the fire. And *I was their firewood*. Every log they threw in the fire burnt readily, steadily, slowly, whilst it also burnt inside me, for this was no sacred fire, but the culmination of the sacrilege they had perpetrated against me and my forest. Good grief, did I hate! I almost suffocated in my own hate, for them and for mankind as a whole.

Then, only then, did I hear millions and millions of cries of pain. It was the millions and millions of trees, not just yews, which man had cut, chopped, slashed, girdled, burned, felled, toppled in his inconsiderate and insane delusions of power and absolute supremacy. At the same time I realised how deaf I had been to all such cries, immersed in self-admiration and oblivious to the suffering of my kindred souls. How self-conceited of me, how insensitive! Amused by whichever triviality, be it man's freakish activities or time travel, I had lost sight of the slaughtering that had been going on for centuries and had taken the lives of millions of yews. How many bows had been made out of our wood? And, if they were so formidable a weapon, why was it that man had not extinguished his own species? No matter how many were killed by the arrows, others would sprout up like mushrooms and take their place. What could I do against the human weed? Perhaps nothing, but hate itself forced me to revive, to rise up again and at least show the world that it takes much more than a humble birch arrow to put an end to a yew.

Among the friars there was one pious young man who had joined them for a rather singular reason.

François had been born in a sunny land to a family of both great traditions and wealth. Being the only son, he was expected to take over his father's power and, like him, to be appreciative of earthly possessions and typical male activities, such as hunting, duelling, womanising. Instead, he displayed a gentle nature, one much bent on contemplation. Furthermore, though not in any way below average in either intelligence or stature, in all fairness it cannot be claimed that he was handsome. To make things worse, at only fourteen years of age he began to lose hair. Within a couple of years he had gone bald. Not only did girls snub him; they mocked him. So, he gave himself to praying.

He prayed and prayed, begging the Blessed Virgin to make his hair grow back. Whether because it was an unprecedented request, or because the Virgin was too busy acceding to other people's supplications, he remained quite hairless.

Rather than addressing his prayers to some other Holiness, he made up his mind to become a friar. The decision horrified his father. Nevertheless, a friar he became. As a man of the cloth, he thought, his prayers would receive preferential treatment.

He prayed and prayed, always to the Blessed Virgin, but still to no avail, for his head continued to look like an overgrown egg. Undaunted, he persuaded himself that participating in the building of a place of worship would prove his goodwill and, as a reward, his hair would grow back. So he came to my forest, helped out in felling me, and then in building the friary.

One early autumn morning he went for a walk between prayers, and happened to trip over me. As he got back on his feet, he gave me a puzzled stare, and then ran frantically back to his Brothers, shouting: "A Miracle, a Miracle!"

"What else have you seen, Brother?" asked the oldest friar, who was quite patient in dealing with François's craving for miracles. The young man, apart from praying, was constantly thinking, but, had one asked, he would have not been sure of what.

"A great Miracle, Father, a great Miracle indeed!" François insisted.

"Come now, Brother. Calm down and explain yourself."

"Why, how could I, of all people, explain a miracle? I can only *believe* in miracles."

The bald friar had a point. So the eldest Brother gathered the other friars, and they all marched to the scene of the miracle.

"What did I tell you? What did I tell you?" asked François, triumphantly.

"I don't know. You mentioned a miracle, but I'm afraid I see no miracle here."

"You don't? You silly goose! Can't you see, can't you all see?" vociferated François, whose fervour had made him forget all due deference. With an emphatic gesture, he made his right hand's forefinger rise up into the air, and then swoop down dramatically, pointing it directly at me. *"There* is the Miracle. *There!"*

"May the Lord be praised," the eldest Brother exclaimed, flabbergasted.

Round what had been the base of my mighty trunk there beckoned a dozen shoots, little stems, little leaves, gazing mystically heavenwards.

"Resurrection, Resurrection!" the friars screamed as they all knelt down before me.

"There's no mistaking it: this is a sign from the Lord Almighty," François said.

"Twelve shoots," one of the friars commented. "Twelve shoots, twelve of us, and the Saviour's twelve disciples."

"We've been sent a signal from Heaven, in the guise of a great Miracle!"

"The greatest Miracle of them all:" the eldest Brother concluded, "Resurrection."

After highly emotional prayers, the friars unanimously decided to build the abbey round me. The resurrected, minuscule

Round what had been the base of my mighty trunk there
beckoned a dozen shoots, little stems, little leaves,
gazing mystically heavenward.
"Resurrection, Resurrection!" – screamed the friars.

yew tree would be at the centre of the cloister, surrounded by an arched arcade where to spend time in pious contemplation of myself, a symbol of their Saviour's Resurrection.

Little by little—it took almost thirty years to complete it—the abbey grew round the cloister court of which I had been made the focal centre. I and the birds which still came to visit me witnessed the coming into being of the building, from its belfry tower to the nave and the sacristy; as well as the more mundane rooms, such as the dormitory, kitchen, cellar and refectory. The friars proved industrious. I even began to think that perhaps their stormy beginnings had misled me, for they really seemed quite tranquil and absorbed by their daily rituals. I often wondered if all that praying could help, as they were inclined to believe? In the end I was content to conclude that, though not provenly useful, it was at least perfectly innocuous.

Besides their spiritual occupations, they diligently tended an orchard on which they relied for part of their food. They even planted a garden for their enjoyment, introducing into it exotic plants which had never grown on my Island, even though I had made their acquaintance in my space travels all over the Earth.

While on the subject. The sad reality that I had been stripped of my global interconnectedness and of my stupendous built-in memory had come as a not entirely unexpected blow. Much as I could not fathom from where they had surfaced, so I could not imagine where they had gone. But gone they were, and for good.

By resorting to growth inhibitors, out of the twelve shoots which had sprouted from my epicormic buds and had impressed the friars so, I elected only one as the stem and trunk-to-be. Its growth thus enhanced, I would resume my pristine single-trunked appearance.

In passing, since later on I will clarify my insight on this subject, I should like to touch on the striking unfairness that is implicit in selecting one shoot—the fittest one—and suppressing the remaining eleven. But this was natural selection, was it not?

When I was beginning to think that the human animal could be, after all, peaceful, for I must admit that the friars were, wine permitting, quite harmless, man went back to his favourite pastime—war.

In two centuries, the abbey was abandoned; then inhabited by friars again; enlarged by additions; and, above all, stormed twice. The first time as a result of a foreign (human) Queen's attempt to curb the local rebels. My Island had fallen a prey to the larger island which lay to the East. It had been divested of its sovereignty and made a colony, so that most of the wood which had been cut down had ended in the clutches of men who did not even speak the language the humans in my Island spoke.

The next time the abbey was attacked, the friars were forced to flee, never to return. A foreign warlord, one Cromwell, had been unleashed against my Island. He adopted a scorched earth policy as his army moved forwards, murdering, destroying, looting, setting houses on fire, in a bid to starve out the rebels that proved all too successful.

When one of his generals reached the abbey, he had his soldiers ravage it and loot it. In their fury of plunder and desecration, they did not seem to take much notice of me, though I had by then grown back into a fairly sizeable tree. Rather than be after my wood and sap, they were after their fellow humans' possessions and blood.

After that the abbey settled into a new role, that of a ruin. Ivy and mice crept into it and kept me company. Many blue and coal tits nestled again in my branches, which cheered me up to some extent.

I no longer felt like the Queen of the Forest. There was no doubt that my prodigious restoration to life had been an unprecedented feat even for a yew, considering my venerable age at the time of my felling. All the woods had acknowledged my triumph over death and had been profoundly moved by it. But the whole natural hierarchy had been challenged, and brought down irreversibly.

All we trees had been deprived of power and had been enslaved by man. We were at his mercy, and he was a merciless tyrant. His thirst for destruction had reached our heretofore undisturbed corner of the world, and it was here to stay, for, across the lake and over the mountains in the direction of the setting sun, there was no more woodland to subdue, but the treeless expanse of the ocean.

These were my dark ages. Though thriving as a relatively young trunk with a crown of branches sheltered by the walls of the cloister court, I could not help thinking about the glorious times in which the yews had virtually no enemy. Somehow, however, I lived on. My roots were still connected with my offspring by way of fungi and even grafts. Many of them were now larger than I was, at least in their aboveground section.

Eventually, a human outcast made of the ruined abbey his nest. "Nest" instead of "dwelling" for this raggedy hermit copied birds and made his resting place out of twigs and dried leaves. Much like my feathered friends, he ate seeds, berries, and even bugs, although seldom. Feeling well at ease in the solitary confines of the abandoned abbey, he made up a legend which concerned me directly so as to keep people away.

"Once," the hermit gravely confessed to the occasional visitor, "a soldier came this way. He was young and haughty. When he saw the yew tree, he decided to cut a branch off it and use it as a staff. I warned him not to do so, but he did not listen. 'You are a filthy beggar,' he said, 'what could you know?' Then he kicked me savagely, for I kept telling him not to touch the yew. When he had kicked me so much that there was no air left in my lungs, he cut off the branch he wanted. But as soon as he tore it away from the tree, the branch dropped blood, and the soldier fell dead on the spot."

Echoed by the people in the region, this ghastly fancy was eventually taken seriously. Once more, fate seemed to plot to keep me alive. As long as man left me alone, I could go on living forever, even though pining over my fondest times, when everything was greener, and full of promise, hope, and treasure.

TWELVE

You may have noticed how, when I speak about mankind and its history, which increasingly encroached on mine, I treat man rather impersonally, at times even offensively. At best, he can be a buffoon whose clownish actions are a source of amusement. At worst, he is the devilish beast that forays, kills, annihilates. Yet, I have voiced these memoirs expressly for you, my kind listeners.

Now, isn't that a striking contradiction? Why, yes. Yet I cannot be accused of being inconsistent, and even less of hypocrisy. If anything, the human species has proved to be inconsistent. But I do not intend to put the subject of our long-standing misunderstandings in these terms, lest I should discomfort the gentlest among you—many women, I trust.

Man is a newcomer that we trees have stopped considering as just one more outlandish animal. Once, he could barely cope with his environment; then he mastered it; eventually, he acquired enough power to devastate it and, sure enough, he did. Possibly inadvertently, probably not quite so innocently.

The religion the holy man brought to my Island greatly encouraged man's predatory nature. Unlike the religion it superseded, this one enthroned man as master of the world and told him to think little or nothing of the other creatures. These had been put there to serve their human master. No teaching could have been more false and unnatural. There was stunning ignorance and short-sightedness on the part of those who put forth these ideas. If I were in a forgiving mood, I might venture that man was blind because he had been blinded, misled by a world-shaking Holy Scripture that did not respect Nature and dislodged every living thing on Earth from its naturally assigned place. However, in conformity with Mother Nature's baffling ambivalence, there have been, and there are, many kind-hearted humans, and these are the ones to whom I pay court.

Perhaps among the just mentioned innocent humans there are some who are unaware of the havoc their predecessors wreaked on us. I myself, due to the peripheral location of my forest, learnt at a relatively late stage of my life exactly what had become of fellow trees and kindred yews.

This is the story within the story of how my Island, which had been a woodland since the retreat of the last ice age, and that is, for almost ten thousand years, within two hundred years became a grassland.

At a time when religion and colonisation made history, the island that had subjugated mine espoused a heretical offshoot of the religion responsible for altering the face of the Earth. There were then new pretexts to go to war: imposing either version of the same religion; colonising distant lands; attaining and maintaining superiority. Whichever the pretext, forests were called upon to fit out the armies of these nations. We yews were cut down by the millions because of the hardness and durability of our wood. Ironically, such features had originally been intended to enhance our survival chances. The yew longbow was the atomic bomb of the Middle Ages. When, to our great relief, firearms bombastically entered the scene, we all rejoiced. Upon hearing of the advent of gunpowder, a son of mine (in human parlance he would be best characterised as being hot-headed) exclaimed: "This is the best news I've ever heard. Now the lowly beasts will still kill one another, but will leave us alone."

It was a promising outlook, but it soon turned into a hellish scenario. Human wars required an army and, even more, a fleet. It was an era of unprecedented maritime rivalry and of enormous wooden ships. Timber supply became intrinsically connected with sea-power and power by and large.

"Timber supply" sounds technical, and is most appropriate. But it says nothing of the systematic and indiscriminate devastation of my Island's forests. Their wood was not used locally, but shipped to the colonising island to the East. Thus my Island became a timber exporter and, in the end, a treeless wilderness.

I saw them all go, one by one, or rather, I heard them go. I heard their cries of agony as they were being cut down and chopped up: hazels, oaks, ashes, elms... Any country aspiring to become a world power had to be a mercantile, seafaring nation. An average gun ship took two thousand well grown trees to make. Bigger ships consumed more and more massive timber. Some required three thousand grown trees; the first-rates, up to four thousand. In acreage, it took fifty acres of woodland to build an average gun ship, and more than double for a first-rate. Then there were freighters, passenger ships, fishing boats, etc.

My Island's woods appeared inexhaustible till they were, in fact, exhausted.

By then, I was dying of a broken heart. What was the point of growing anew and winning battles against time and the odds of a long existence when foreign visitors touring my Island would invariably remark, "The most striking aspect of the landscape here is the absence of trees; they seem to have been relegated to private parks"?

Little if any comfort in that tamed setting either.

We yews, after having been venerated by the ancient people's religion, and at least regarded as symbolically relevant by the new religion, were now being pruned, trimmed and clipped into geometrical figures and grotesque forms. Thus prescribed topiary art, the latest gardening fashion. These gardens were analogous to animals' zoos, yet worse for, no matter how confined a beast may be, its natural form is not altered by man. In our case, not only did man plant us in his "formal" gardens here or there at will, but he also mutilated us so as to appear "graceful", or to portray, through a studious pruning of our branches, something other than ourselves, such as a rabbit, an obelisk, a sphere, and so on. Not to mention how many us were regimented into hedges.

"We've come full circle," I would ponder, bitterly. "Man used to be our helpless clown. The situation is now reversed."

But, as the wisest among you must know, there is no single true story. In the midst of this deforestation, or, away with euphemisms, our holocaust, one could have detected a few encouraging signals, provided he or she looked keenly, and with a magnifying glass.

Not as a deliberate decision made so as to halt our exploitation, but as a matter-of-course transition to steel ships, the era of the wooden ship entered its twilight. Furthermore, the founding on my Island of a society, whose aim was the fostering of forestry and especially reforestation, appeared quite promising. Between 1766 and 1806 twenty-five million trees were planted thanks to such a society, and gold medals awarded to people who planted a great number of trees. Most of these foreseeing humans had understood that conservation was the way of the future, and that there would be no future without us trees. Their objectives, therefore, only accidentally happened to tally with ours, by which I mean, the will to survive.

This was the same sort of man that, in 1786, had shot down my Island's last wolf. Times were not ripe yet for comprehensive ecological conservation. Trees, however, were not merely useful but downright indispensable; as such, they had to be kept in constant supply. On the other hand, wolves were perceived as only harmful, and were therefore exterminated.

Owing to its beauty, which was still miraculously unspoilt by man, the area in which I had been living for eighteen hundred years had become a favourite destination for adventurous travellers, the forefathers of modern-day tourists. They came from within and without my Island, and brought along appreciation and interest in local lore.

One beautiful morning the sun finally came out of retirement after a month of nearly uninterrupted rain, and an elegant gentleman made his way to the ruined, ivy-clad abbey. It was not as unusual an occurrence as it would have been thirty springs before, but still infrequent enough to alert my attention.

This gentleman, a foreigner, was accompanied by a rosy-cheeked little girl. I immediately felt her disarming candour and gentle heart transpire from beneath her skin, and listened carefully to the words they exchanged in their musical tongue.

"Pray tell me, Claire," her father asked, "do trees speak? Do they remember? Do they think?"

"At night they speak to each other," answered the little girl, aglow with smiles for her father, "and during the day too."

"Well then, why don't we hear them?"

"I hear them whisper 'Sh… Sh… Sh…'"

"Couldn't that be the wind?"

"Yes." She laughed.

"Then they *don't* speak."

"No, no, no. The trees tell the leaves to tell the wind to blow."

"Then they only speak when the wind blows?"

"That's right."

"And when there's no wind?"

"They sleep."

"And what if the wind never comes, my beautiful ray of sunshine?"

"They sleep for a hundred years till it comes."

"And why don't they speak our language?"

"They speak *their* language, daddy dear."

"And we need a… magic hat to understand it?"

"Not me, only you."

"I see. Then you understand their language, don't you?"

"Of course, everything they say."

"And what is this magnificent yew tree telling you?"

The little girl with the golden tresses gazed at me. Then she smiled, and said: "She's telling me that she likes me."

"Really now?"

How could her father even remotely imagine the truth in the words of his little girl?

"She's telling me something else," Claire continued, her eyes caressing my stalwart trunk, still dripping with rain. "Would you like to know what?"

"By all means," her father answered half-facetiously.

"She's telling me that she's lonely and that she'd like to have more company."

... immediately felt her disarming candour
and gentle heart transpire from beneath her skin.

Blessed little herald of truth! When I think back I can still see her, gorgeous, pure little thing, speaking such words of wisdom. In her I trace the dawning of a sense of hope, hope in the human species as a green race, a kindly race.

My hopes have been dashed since, on repeated occasions. But at least I had proof that a human heart could nurture kind feelings, particularly when beating peacefully in the chest of a woman. Evidently, a million years of procreation, rearing and protection of their young could not be forgotten. Just as a million years of hunting, fighting, killing, and manifold predation have consequences for men.

I had been begetting offspring for centuries and knew that there is no loftier gift to be had on Earth, particularly when procreation is not somewhat automatic, as with fungi or ferns, but meant, sought, desired.

The railway came to the edges of my forest. For once, rather than bringing crazed loggers, it brought romantic nature lovers. Hotels were built, and with them a town, which sprouted up in haste like a birch. Castles were either turned into lodgings for wealthy visitors or hotels equipped with modern conveniences were built nearby. Then I began to suspect that man would no longer cut us down. I became sure of that when one Queen Victoria, apparently the most powerful woman on Earth then, visited my grounds and, among other things, supervised the commemorative planting of some oaks. She could have chosen yews instead, but in any case planting was far more desirable than felling.

For a change, the people in my corner of the world had something to sell: scenery, and I was a part of it. Not that I minded, for I had seen worse times and had no argument with, but only compassion for, the local populace. Like all the other

Islanders, some thirty years before, they had been stricken by a devastating famine which was partly caused by the above mentioned Queen whose light-hearted policy in dealing with the crisis, or rather the policy of her cabinet of ministers, had proved utterly inadequate. And to think that such an immense tragedy could have been largely alleviated or altogether avoided if there had been a responsible governmental commitment.

I heard of men, women and children dying by the thousands of hardships, cold, deprivations. At least the local humans had scenery to sell, and, thanks to the revenues thus generated, they somehow pulled through.

A quaint town grew round the vestiges of history and the beauty of my forest. More people came from afar to admire the scenery.

Early in this century, the landowners who had possessed themselves of my naturally inherited grounds donated them to the state, which later on incorporated them with some adjacent land into a national park. This marked the institutionalisation of a change in mood in man: the coming into being of national parks, wildlife reserves, natural sanctuaries all over the Earth. In them lay the foundations of a new attitude. Perhaps inevitably it was still man-centred, for the parks were instituted for the enjoyment of the human visitors. But they were the first, tangible, long-overdue signs of mankind coming to its senses.

THIRTEEN

As I gaze at the lake, at its many bays and little islands, at the formal grounds with many exotic trees wedged into the preserved wilderness around me, I see the whole place teeming with tourists. They come from faraway lands and presume to capture what they see on film, videotape and what not. Sometimes there are as many tourists as blue tits.

Not that I mind this human category. It's thanks to tourists and things conceived for their delight that I am now a national monument; that tree watchers and botanists alike come to me and my woodland with earnest intentions; that I have a protective railing round me which prevents lovers from carving their initials into my bark with a pocket knife. None of them even remotely fathoms my age, which is four times what dendrochronologists and historians estimate. None of them can imagine all I have witnessed, endured and done during my long life, let alone my stupendous memory. Yet, they are cheerful and welcome company.

Only a couple of centuries ago the pure yew woodland my offspring formed in the course of two millennia would have conjured up visions of gloom and doom, wicked witches and black-hearted wolves. Today, though somebody still maintains that it is a "weird" place, I hear praise about its rarity, its dense shade, its uninterrupted carpet of moss.

The imported and weedy rhododendron has been extensively uprooted and burned, and no longer constitutes a threat. The Sika deer are under control too.

These dainty animals, imported over a century ago from a distant island at the other end of the Earth, looked perfectly harmless, almost like a scaled-down replica of the majestic native deer. But they soon displayed a hideous alimentary preference: they loved to chew yew bark, the same toxic bark which is lethal to most animals. Thousands of years ago man had learned to girdle us, or strip us of our bark in order to kill us. Recently, however, he has unlearned this feat, or at least the enlightened representatives of the human species have. It was ironic that an imported quadruped would pick up where man had finally left off.

Particularly vulnerable patches where seedlings are attempting to grow into saplings and eventually trees have been fenced to prevent access to these bark-devourers. Other sizeable specimens have been individually fenced—two daughters and a handsome son of mine, so handsome that, though I never quite saw him, he reminds me of his father, or of the way I always imagined he looked.

There is concern in the botanical community, for the yew woodland has apparently come to a standstill, with no yew seedlings to be found anywhere. Consequently, it is inferred that the yew woodland is doomed because it is no longer reproducing.

But pure yew stands, that is, woodlands composed exclusively of yew trees, are anomalies. You now know how this one came into being. Perhaps I ought not to have made a clean sweep of all the oaks in my forest, perhaps I ought to have allowed some of them to grow side by side with us. I regret having been heavy-handed, not only because I cleared my woods of such a fundamental life-sustaining tree, but also because I inadvertently sent out the wrong message to my offspring. By clearing their way to me and modelling their conduct after mine, they have pushed all other trees off to the edges of the woods.

If they do not reproduce it is because they miss the company of other species, which in turn support a greater variety of flora and fauna, particularly birds and small mammals. At any rate, there is no need to be frenetic. You now realise how long-lived yews are, or at least can be, when loggers are kept at a distance. Eventually one in a thousand seeds will become a seedling, then a sapling, finally a tree. That's all it takes, provided the chain saws rust away in some deserted shed.

As for the will to live, not only have I inculcated it into my offspring, but I have always called it "the joy of being alive."

But what do these concerns mean to the well-intentioned tourist who, leaning on the iron railing round my trunk, is staring at me from down below, in the old cloister, focusing his camera lens on my crown of branches? When the tourist is a woman, things are generally better. A plaque hung upon the northern wall of the ambulatory, while relating only a fraction of my story, informs her that I am a female too. A special connection is established at once.

Sometimes I indulge in a semi-serious hypothesis. Suppose the universe has come about through the doing of some creative agent. Then, judging from how life as we know it appears to be, such an agent must have been creating during an untimely moment of phenomenal senselessness, or downright dementia. Surely a cat or a frog could have come up with a smoother world, one not plagued by so many absurdities. But, so much for that. I'm afraid this may start to sound like senile babbling, so let me drop it and move on.

Mrs. and Mr. Birdwatcher; Mrs. and Mr. Treewatcher: thank you. Thank you for coming here; thank you for watching me and the birds chirping away all over me; thank you for having restored some self-esteem. What a foolish thing it is to analyse life! We'd better live it and get on with it. After all, in life one normally wants to find today, and cares not to lose tomorrow. Myself first and foremost. Now, I suppose I want to find tomorrow and care no more about today. *And it's infuriating.*

I was always the first one to reawaken after winter; always the last one to fall asleep, reluctantly, well into autumn, remember? Indeed, for almost two thousand years I was the Island's most partially dormant tree. Whenever temperature allowed, I roused from sleep, even if for a few hours, and put slumber off as long as I could. Can you blame me? I am still immersed in sheer beauty: mountains, hills, moors; the lake's rippled waters; leaves on the turn (I can see the oaks across the lake from here); red squirrels climbing, leaping, falling, blown away by gusty winds; and twittering gangs of birds, too many species—and many visiting from distant countries—to mention them all, plucking my berries, which I surrender with *gusto*. May they eat them and carry them off to near and faraway lands.

This spectacle I beheld when I was a tiny seedling. The same spectacle, give or take a monastery here, a castle there, my abbey, all in ruin and all dear to me by now, I behold today, almost two thousand years later. I loved it then, love it still. I could never fall out of love with it. Moreover, it is now dotted with hundreds of my offspring, by whom my love is echoed and amplified. Sometimes I wonder whether I could go on enjoying this spectacle eternally. It is worth it, and I need not fear man any longer. The greatest tree pathogen is now my greatest protector. Why, yes, I am protected, and not just by the iron railing round my trunk. The curator of the national park drops by quite often.

He is a personable chap, the husband of a genial woman, and the father of five children whom he sometimes brings along. He checks on my state of health periodically and reports it annually to the Office of Public Works. I would not be surprised if he too believed in the legend about the mortal danger involved in touching me.

Once, some dried up branches of mine had to be sawn off. He hired a tree surgeon from another county and, before the pruning got under way, whispered something so that only I could hear it.

"We're doing this for your own good. It's a minor pruning and we will *not* cut *any* live branches."

Although he discovered it years ago, he has never shown any intention to touch it. "It" is a natural hazel bonsai which grows from one of my limbs. A squirrel forgot the nut there, there was some leaf mould, it sprouted, and now I host a little bush. No harm from it, and little growing prospect for it either, due to the obvious lack of soil. But the curator won't tear the hazel off me. A credulous man? Perhaps, though I know he will not believe just anything.

How do I know that? A few months ago, an eminent scientist from the New World stopped by on his way to the Continent, and asked the curator to guide him through a tour of the park, particularly to that "legendary" yew tree he had heard so much about.

When the two of them reached the cloister of the abbey, the scientist was absorbed by the content of a recent paper, which he was to outline in a lecture at a prestigious university. He was going over it with the curator, and this is what I heard.

"As you know," the eminent man of science said as they stepped into the shady cloister and leant on the railing round me, "Mars is believed to be lifeless. But it may be possible to transform it into a planet suitable for plants, and, arguably, also for humans."

"Is that so?"

"It is. You see, it has become increasingly clear that humans can alter the environment on a planetary scale." (Tell me about it!) "We can so successfully manipulate our terrestrial environment, that it is not inconceivable for me to propose that man can turn Mars into another Earth, can 'terraform' it, by utilising indigenous Martian resources."

"'Terraform'," the curator thought, "now, that's a good one."

Citing directly from the paper he must have memorised, the scientist continued: "We could change the planet's environmental parameters, such as the distribution of volatiles; the surface temperature as well as pressure; the atmospheric composition and opacity; the planetary albedo and, lastly, the humidity and precipitation. Now, the amount of sunlight on Mars is much more than needed for photosynthesis, so light would not be a limiting factor. Some oxygen is required by plants, as you know, for aerobic mitochondrial respiration, though it appears that plants prefer oxygen levels well below the current values. Nitrogen is required by all organisms, and recent work indicates that bacteria can fix nitrogen at pressures of..."

He went on and on, quoting formulæ of "thermal balance", and expressing outlandish concepts such as "desorption of the Martian regolith CO_2 on heating", etc.

The curator and I tuned out simultaneously. Then the souls of the people buried in the graveyard next to the abbey, among them three poets who would have turned in their graves had it not started to rain the way it can rain here—torrentially. The two men left the abbey, not on particularly good terms because, when asked for an opinion about this ambitious project, the caretaker replied: "Years ago I saw a B movie on the same subject."

Good for you, my kind caretaker. Well done! "Terraforming" Mars, what nerve! At first, I rather liked the idea of space-age humans migrating en masse to a distant planet. Why, I still feared them, notwithstanding their change in mood, and here was the possibility to see them off, once and for all, and to have the Earth all to ourselves. How marvellous! But then I was abruptly brought back to a grim reality. Plants were supposed to go up there first so as to render, in time, the planet habitable for humans. What a horrifying *déjà vu*. Not again, please! Couldn't we just part our ways? I guess not. We plants thrive without humans. It is humans who cannot do without us.

The underlying misunderstanding, though, is a more profound one. My dear and kind friends, I ask you: What is so great about Earth, and life as we know it on Earth, to inspire some of us to export it all the way to another planet? Should we also export life's inherent strife? Its harshness? Its ambivalence? Or rather, should it be a better place? One in which we may do away with all the redundancies you, mother nature, have burdened us with? One in which I would not need to bear thousands and thousands of berries to see but a few seedlings, if any, grow out of them. Perhaps man would not need millions of spermatozoa to fertilise but one woman's egg.

Why not conceive a world in which every seed turns into a tree, in which for every sperm there is one egg? Then all species would multiply and prosper lovingly, unfettered, unchallenged.

An unearthly place? Yes. An unnatural place? No! Why should it be unnatural? Did it ever occur to you, mother nature, that competition and "natural" selection may well be unnatural? Why, there must be a better place, somewhere. One with no ambivalence, where the local Mother Nature is ever kindly, never merciless. Forgive me, if you can. You may find me ungrateful, even blasphemous. Why should I, highborn and privileged both by birth and chance, complain about life's unfairness? Precisely for that: can you even vaguely imagine how many times I've asked myself, from the height of my grand and age-old existence, "Why, why all this strife, why all this grievous strife?" You may answer, mockingly, "Go tell a wolf to become a lamb and graze on grass." And not that grass would particularly care for that either...

Well, I don't know, I can't fathom a way out. It's not up to me, and even less so up to disorderly man—let us all be delivered from his farfetched projects. But the stars up in the heavens seem to gild our nights without strife, at peace with themselves, with one another and with us. No, do not expect to be called Mother Nature anymore, for competition, rivalry, strife, should never have been disguised as "natural". If this is all you've been able to come up with in millions upon millions of years, then you're a mediocre mother. *You, you* unfit for your role, *you* unearthly, *you* unforgiving, *you* unnatural! Mother nature, do not take umbrage if I speak so frankly, or do, if you wish, I don't care. I'm an old lady, and my great age entitles me to take liberties. All things considered, I've had a wonderful life. Thanks. But most beings can't even claim to have lived a decent life, let alone wonderful. So take me, if you will. Make me be hit by lightning, stir up an earthquake, melt down the icy poles and drown me...

...Or try, if only for a moment, to imagine a kindlier place, one where every grain of pollen pollinates a flower; where all that which could be born, is born—no competitors, no competition, no limits whatsoever to Life. The question is not, "Why were we born?" but, "Why should we die?"

But then, can you devise such a place? A great star somewhere, a strifeless place of limitless bounty? Who knows? Perhaps, if we all thought about it ceaselessly, then the amplified resonance of our thinking might make this place come into existence. Perhaps, it already exists.

You humans, you, the ones who in ten thousand years have domesticated the Earth, don't you dare believe that it is governed by eternal laws. There are only habits, and the inertia caused by force of habit. Things come into being, we all have.

Look at my invisible heart, listen to my silent heart, as I near my last breath. Certainly, I'm very different from a hot-blooded animal. But in this supreme moment it doesn't matter, I don't care, for what I've narrated to you has come from the heart—the very heart I do not have.

For the first time since my very early, very green years, I feel love for everything and for everyone again. This world is a battleground where an unconditional love for everything and everyone does not belong. Therefore, it's time I issued forth on a pathway of deliverance.

To all of you I bequeath my testimony. Somewhere in the aforesaid I hope you find some solace, some inspiration, some truth. Centuries ago, the Green Man also left the Earth. But his message, I now know, lives on. And there is hope that plant and human will join in consciousness.

In bidding you a fond farewell, my kind and dear human listeners, and plants, and animals, as many as there are species, though satiated by a generous life, I shall indulge in a sort of after-dinner delight: the last setting of the sun over the lake, the last hours of a night full of promise.

These memoirs I have voiced will be collected in a book. Paper is made of wood, pages are leaves. There are now only five leaves left. When you will have unhurriedly turned over the last leaf, it shall have dawned once more, and I will have issued forth, skywards, aloft and yonder.

These memoirs I have voiced will be collected in a book.
Paper is made of wood, pages are leaves. There are now only
five leaves left. When you will have unhurriedly turned over the
last leaf, it will have dawned once again
and I will have issued forth, skyward, aloft and yonder.

Author's Compendium

Apropos of *The Story of Yew,* the late Aidan Brady, director of the National Botanical Gardens in Glasnevin, Dublin, wrote, *inter alia:* "Only the supreme optimist would have attempted to write a novel by this title." On the other hand, what callous, thick human being could stand in front of a patriarch of an ancient tree unmoved, feeling nothing? An ancient tree, a "living monument". The word "monument" derives from the Latin *monere,* meaning at once to remember *and* to warn. Voicing the unvoiced, I realised, had to do with *both* remembering and...warning. Who? Us, we conspicuously short-sighted worldings. Hence the title *The Story of Yew,* in which the pun is, indeed, intended.[1] The story to be told is that of you all, us all, *it* all—the story streaming down to us from a botanically extraordinary tree enwrapped in history, legend and religious significance.

I used to sense that I would have to be an octogenarian just to approach such a lofty subject, and then treat it with no fewer than two thousand pages. But then two considerations altered my position. Did I have any guarantee that I would turn eighty someday? How much spark, dynamism, and ambition is, under normal circumstances, left to an octogenarian?

The philosophical point of departure, or stumbling block, was that most puzzling aphorism by which a young and idiosyncratic Wittgenstein had elected to conclude his *Tractatus Logico-Philosophicus:* "About that of which we cannot speak, we must remain silent."

It was, indeed, a dilemma, and for a while I despaired, fearing not to be able to grasp what might well be the ungraspable. Notwithstanding that, I researched furiously and exhaustively; contacted world-class botanists and naturalists, and began to correspond and meet with them, above all with Alan Mitchell, the leading authority on trees of the British Isles (who was then to guide me through all botanical aspects in the book); and repeatedly journeyed to England, Scotland, and even Ireland, though the number and

---

[1] If language, as an interphase, is to have a role in gnosis, a play on words—a *sprach spiel*—might be seen in the perspective of an "arcane" philological contrivance, journeying through Cabalistic and emblematic constructs, through occult etymologies and Sufi decodings, as if in a regress to a pre-Babel, universally meaningful state.

size of yews in the latter country could hardly contend with the former ones. I was moved on English and Scottish soil by the sight and contact with many an ancient yew. But it wasn't enough. It snapped on me whilst in Ireland. The story of the yew is the story of the World Tree[2], of *all* trees, and of us, anthropoid mammals. Where else would one find the palpable sense of bereavement of a whole Island that *was* a woodland, *is* a grassland, but in Ireland?[3] Ancient underground fungal interconnections had lost their original use, but I felt they still functioned, broadcasting, ever so subvocally for those who *would* listen, the plight of all trees. Vestiges of massive tree fellings, girdlings, burnings...

On my way back from Ireland, I knew it was time to harness my *vox humana* and speak through it the words of the yew.

How would I structure the memoirs? In a diametrically opposite fashion to that which I had assumed I would use. First of all, I was far from being an octogenarian. Secondly, it would not be a drawn-out marathon, but a concise and eminently rhapsodic autobiography/ecofable. Every chapter would be a rhapsody of a parable, with a message, artfully developed. Every character would be an archetype, emblematic of something of universal significance. Chapters would grow more involved as the yewess grew older, but I clearly saw that, in tune with Wittgenstein, as well as with good literary sense, it is better to leave the readers asking for more pages than to drown them in endless babble.

What follows is a document of the genesis of this book and a chapter-by-chapter guide to its influences and implications.

FOREWORD

Of all the terms I could use to indicate a piece of information placed before the first chapter for the benefit of the reader—preface, premise, prelude, preamble, prologue, introduction, etc.—I selected "foreword", the most straightforward. It tells of the tone of the Foreword itself. It acquaints the

---

[2] I need not venture, here, into comparative taxonomy, but it must be owned that there exist striking similarities between the Taxus and the Podocarpus, whose natural range spans over the Tropics and the Southern Hemisphere. Then, since the Taxus is found all over the Northern Hemisphere, we can rightly claim that we are dealing with a plant whose plasticity makes it the true citizen of the world.

From a mythological standpoint, the World Tree, also called Cosmic Tree (and Tree of Knowledge in some traditions), as the centre of the world, is a widespread motif among various preliterate and literate peoples, in all continents. It defines the human/profane condition in relation to the divine/sacred realm. Esoteric treatises have been written on the subject from antiquity onwards. The revelations therein are consistently startling. The interested reader may use as a starting point P. L. Travers's *In Search Of The World Tree*, published in the magazine *Parabola*, in the Fall 1999 issue.

[3] Ireland as an emblem of a world-wide alarmingly familiar trend—that of desertification.

reader without delay with what the story is about: the autobiography of an age-old yew tree. I then ask the listeners, as the tree will *tell*, not *write* her story (as a genuine hearth-side storyteller), to set aside "their assumptions on the superiority of the human race." Plainly put: let the yew tree take you by the hand and tell you what is worth listening to. So as to bridge the gap between humans and trees, the yew has employed our language.[4]

ONE

"The first note is invariably the trickiest note."[5] It is the most obvious "statement", as it interrupts the preceding silence unequivocally; yet, while it must say enough to capture the listener's attention, it cannot overdo it. It occurred to me that I could begin from the end, and that is, the age. "Twenty-four thousand seven hundred and forty moons ago, today:" roughly two-thousand years. Too much for a beginning? Not really; the narrating yew immediately scales down and flashes back to her earliest recollections.

I must confess that I was not unmindful of the masterful childhood evocation by which begins *David Copperfield*. Here too I tried to permeate the first pages, or leaves, with a sense of wonder, and delight, the same wonder and delight that come to a happy youth. There are glimpses of Thoreau and Whitman. *Life in the Woods* and *Leaves of Grass* are, of course, inspiring texts, for their human sensitivity and stylistic abnormality alike. Everything that does not quite fit into a contemporary fashion or style usually lasts when all other trends have long been buried.

TWO

In the early chapters, everything seems to be fine, in its proper place and at the right time. Yet, from the very outset, it is apparent that the yewess is not quite like her many brothers and sisters. She is possessed of a lively curiosity that, with the passing of the centuries, will become unquenchable thirst for knowledge. She knows that she is endowed with an immense, congenital memory, yet is denied access to it (presumably because she is too small and immature). So Mother Nature sends her go-betweens of knowledge, usually humble but omniscient insects. Through them and her

---

[4] Language means far more to me than a mere vehicle of communication. In it, I detect a sense of indwelling otherworldliness which reaches beyond Wittgenstein, George Steiner and all Western linguists. What should be made of the Hopi language, destitute of past or future tenses or concepts? Of Esperanto, which is based on Turkish (!) grammar? Or of Arabic, the most precise and ancient of the Semitic languages, built upon mathematical principles, and philologically millennia more archaic than, for instance, Hebrew?

[5] As Keith Jarrett said, in reference to the first note of his piano improvisations, at a concert I attended in Los Angeles.

biological mother she comes to know much about the forest and the yew's place in it.

I must pause here for a moment and refer to a book which has cast quite an influence on the shaping of the memoirs. About 2100 years ago there lived in Rome a peculiar and elusive man, Titus Lucretius Carus, whose great didactic poem, *De Rerum Natura* has outlived him, Rome, the Holy Roman Empire, and will be read well into the Third Millennium. In six succinct books compounded of solid reasoning, soaring imagination, and noble poetry, he expounds all knowledge and wisdom with the objective to enable man to attain peace of mind and detachment from earthly things. Some passages from it are so timelessly true and hauntingly beautiful, I felt I had chanced (though I hadn't, really, for it was one of the few Latin texts I felt any fond memories for from my years at the *lycée*, and therefore it was a conscious *repêchage*) on a text that transcends its author and times.

The yewess grows by a lake[6], and a handsome one at that. It is not a casual choice. Ancient Irish poets believed that the brink of water was always a place where *eicse*—"wisdom", "knowledge"—would be revealed.[7] I investigated the etymology of Irish (Celtic) words such us *iubher, yew; fidnemed,* possibly a sanctuary, *Bile Tortan,* and its mystic centre without dimension, etc. Eoin Neeson's *A History of Irish Forestry* was of great help. In it, among many valuable inklings of forgotten mores, I found an ancient hierarchy of the forest, after which I modelled my own, which the old mother yew related to her precocious daughter. It placed the yew at the top of the tree hierarchy.

Reassured by the comforting news, the yewess looks forward to gaining girth, stature and, eventually, the reins of command. She was the princess of the forest and destined to succeed to her mother as the Queen.[8] But for the time being, the little yewess, a few springs old, is utterly enthralled by her surroundings, the fellow stationary plants and the many mobile animals, the sheer beauty of the place. When some clouds of pollen come wafting by, and when she is told that they are not clouds, but her father, she

---

[6] The beginning is imbued with a fairy tale atmosphere. All geographical notions would be sorely out of place at this stage. Indeed, throughout the memoirs I will give as scant topographical intelligence as the context will allow. Only later on will it become apparent that the soil on which the yewess grows is Irish soil. That is because the yewess truly feels to be at the centre of the universe and to be the princess of such a universe. Ironically, it will be thanks to her rather peripheral location that the invading armies will spare her time and time again.

[7] I should not dwell here on the esoteric meanings to be found in ancient Ireland at the time in which our tree was beginning to grow. Suffice it to say that I undertook an extensive research into ancient Celtic beliefs both in Ireland and in present-day UK, regarding trees, forests, religions, beliefs, rituals... often arriving at startling revelations.

[8] A central theme in the yewess's life: hierarchy. And tradition. In other words, the obligations of excellence. Considering that another equally central theme is rebellion, in this ambivalence lies some of the complexity of the heroine's personality.

is delighted. Life is wonderful, and her mother is *all that she needs, all that she wants, and that's all.*[9]

THREE

At some time between her twentieth and thirtieth spring, the yewess finds out about "them", i.e., men. "Men" more so than "man", meaning mankind, as her first glimpse of humans beholds the drama of male head-hunters and their captured victim. From now onwards, she will decidedly have a preference for female beings. Much later on will it become apparent that she places on women her only hope for mankind to come to grips with reality and mend its murderous ways.

But there is only surprise at the strange cruelty of the first men she ever sees. These new animals, men and women, are intriguing beasts who can provide welcome entertainment to the woods.

The she-wolf will impart alarming details about this novel "man-creature". Nevertheless, the yewess will still be more than hesitant to fear man in the least. Although the whole forest echoes with:

> Man is wicked
> wicked, wicked...

her fears are allayed by a druid.[10] In his informal ceremony by mother yew (they have elected this place as the tribe's sacred grove) he makes it clear that the yews are worshipped by these people. Mother yew tells her that they have understood that the Spirit belongs to trees, and particularly to yew trees.

Consequently, man cannot be such a monster, ponders the young yewess. After all, he has placed the monarch of the forest, the yew tree, at the centre of his religion. And, moreover, the corpse of the slain man is not where it had lain. The woods' waste disposal has been at work and the victim has gone back to earth, just like all other animals. He too appears to be transient.

The yewess is young, and green, in awe of her surroundings. As many raw youths, she feels, somehow, invulnerable. She cannot even conceive that wounds and blows can and do come.[11] In these early chapters, there is still a sense of delight and wonderment.

---

[9] Some lyrics borrowed from a song by the Waterboys.

[10] By the word "druid" I do not mean "priest" in any sense, but rather a man of knowledge and of power. Irish druids in particular were magi, a step above any of the modern-day scientific priesthood counterpart.

[11] *"Los golpes de la vida,"* (the blows of life) as the Peruvian poet Vallejo calls the tragedies in one's life.

FOUR

The premise for this chapter is an oddity: the famous Roman IX Hispana "missing" Legion. After having been stationed in Britannia for quite some time, it vanished from the face of the earth. I thought I might link this historical oddity with the Roman non-conquest of Hibernia, i.e., Ireland. The yewess is growing (122 years old) and her story, unfolding, enfolds history. Stakes are now higher, as if in preparation for her future as queen of the woods. It seems appropriate that she would witness the event that determined the *non*-invasion of Ireland.

The chapter's hero, or archetype, is one Aeneas, the son of a ruthless Roman tribune who projects his ambitions on his unambitious son. The very name he bestowed on his son is burdened with history.

By this time, Virgil's *The Aeneid*[12] was a smashing success throughout the Roman Empire. Yielding to Agustus's request, the poet had set out to celebrate the birth of Rome in Homeric fashion and, in everyone's opinion, had succeeded triumphantly. Nobody seemed to heed the epic's more ambiguous antihero implications which make it dear to modern readers. Or its central theme of constant and woeful uprooting. Aeneas is forced again and again to pluck up roots and move on towards the destination set out for him by fate, *not* by personal choice. Aeneas must constantly suffer. He, the uprooted hero, even becomes, for Queen Dido, a carrier of uprootedness.

But *my* Aeneas will *not*. He will no longer be an exile (in Latin: *exsul,* means "from the soil"). Unlike the original Aeneas, mine will refuse to be a *fato profugus,* an exile by force of destiny, an utterly displaced person. That is highly symbolic. Indeed, it is the first instance of that other recurrent theme—rebellion. The very rebellion that the Fairy Maid embraces. She decides that she will be a snare for men no longer, even if that is what she is supposed to do forever. The yewess encourages rebellion to one's fate, and admires Aeneas and the Fairy Maid for daring to rebel against a fate that had been set out for them.

I was inspired to this theme of rebellion by an irresistible old Irish folk song, *The Raggle Taggle Gypsy.* Some may object to the association, Latin classical poetry x Irish folklore, but the song blends beautifully with the learned poetry of Virgil. It tells of a woman who, on the spur of the moment, leaves her lawfully wedded powerful lord, his money, land, house and arrogance for a raggle taggle gypsy-o! How could she leave her husband for... *that*? Her reply:

---

[12] Virgil was not only an illustrious classical poet, of course. His earlier works were virtually agricultural treatises in poetry, with every farming detail to be found in them, from how and when to prune different trees and shrubs to how to be a successful beekeeper. An accomplished agronomist himself, he could have been a scientist by profession had science, or what we mean today by this term, existed. His love for plants and nature always exceeded his love for literature, no matter how keen it was to become.

What care I for my house and my land
What care I for my money-o?
I'd rather have a kiss from the yellow gypsy's lips
I'm away with the raggle taggle gypsy-o!

We live in a world so infected by avarice and greed, it is refreshing to know that there existed and perhaps still exist women who will give up everything for the sake of a wild romance. At its core there is much idealism, the very idealism that inspires indomitability.

So, Aeneas is finally sown into a suitable soil; the Fairy Maid gives up her deceiving ways in exchange for eternal devotion to the umpteenth man she was supposed to cast at the bottom of the lake. Greed is the loser, as the invasion fails and Aeneas's father is sentenced; and love triumphs, as thousands of fairies dissuade the Roman soldiers from any belligerent intent, and lure them into befriending and then marrying local women.

FIVE

The yewess is by now four centuries old. She has become a keen observer of the woods, singling out the pretty strawberry tree as her bosom friend[13]. She has also noticed that her mother is ageing, but is not worried about this, as every organism in the forest seems to be fond of the great matriarch. But she would like to know... more, her curiosity being, as ever, insatiable. Soon enough she will be visited by one of Nature's last go-betweens: a slug who will recount the religious war that is raging over the Island.

The transition from the Celtic to the Christian religion will be stunningly rapid, but not entirely smooth. Luckily, the yewess will be reassured by knowing that even this new religion holds the yew tree in the greatest esteem, though holy places will be removed from the sacred groves and will be now made by human hands. Seamus Heaney has written an essay about this abrupt desacralisation of nature, *The God in the Tree*. According to man's new religion—one that came from an arid, nearly treeless land—the god was not to be found in the tree anymore. Rather, in an entirely manmade place of worship, a church.[14] Why was it that Saint Patrick kept the yew tree in a pre-eminent position within his imported religion? Pope Gregorius Magnus was a great promoter of missionaries, and

---

[13] Native to the Mediterranean, the strawberry tree (Arbutus unedo) is, oddly, also endemic to South West Ireland, especially near Killarney. This longevous evergreen is believed to be a relic from before the last ice age.

[14] The Roman historian Tacitus, when writing about Welsh druids and their rites, remarked that they had no temples, for "they thought it absurd to portray like a man or circumscribe within the walls of a house the Being who created the immensity of the heavens." Druidical rites were mostly performed within a sacred grove.

shrewd enough to teach them to incorporate local beliefs and rituals into the Christian religion. Exactly what happened with Patrick.

I have been partially reconsidering this stance which is perhaps too harsh in regard to the Church. It is a fact that for three hundred years Christians were persecuted, tortured and put to death in the most excruciating ways (one among them all: covered with pitch and then set ablaze as human torches so as to illuminate the coliseum where more fellow Christians were being fed to the lions for the entertainment of the masses). And at the core of Christianity there is a kindliness unknown to most previous religions. Yet, no-one is to forget that at the very beginning of the King James Bible it is written, when God is speaking to the first man and woman:

> Be fruitful, and increase, fill the earth, and subdue it:
> and have dominion over the fish in the sea, the birds of
> the air, and every living thing that moves on the earth.
> (Genesis 1:28)

This injunction encouraged man's predatory nature. We are all beholding the disaster Western man in particular has caused on this earth which he would not respect anymore, but subdue and ravish.

No wonder I end the chapter with the famous banishing of the snakes from Ireland. The version I adopt was told to me by one (venerably old) Danny Cronin, a mine of Kerry lore, over many a pint of Guinness in a pub in Killarney. I loved it and inserted it almost verbatim.

According to legend, St. Patrick banished Ireland's last snake in Serpent Lake, in the proximity of Killarney, where the yewess grows. It is meant to be a cherished, symbolic date. I view it as the beginning of hardship for nature in the Island.

SIX

Birth and death punctuate earthly life in a most conclusive fashion. Our yewess, by now the most attractive tree in the forest, had presumed to be a keen observer of nature. Instead, she had entirely misinterpreted the signs of her mother's impending death—and there were quite a few of them. She is so utterly "heartbroken" that for thirty years she simply refuses to grow.

Yews are seen to behave quite erratically in their growth patterns. Sometimes growth can accelerate with age, or diminish, or stall for years. I used this peculiarity of theirs as a self-induced coma, an attempted suicide. The yewess is not only grieved by the mourning: she is angry at herself for not having seen what had been so evident to everyone else in the forest. Guilt-ridden, she can hardly tolerate her own foolishness and vanity. Bereavement sets in; living on feels intolerable. So, life is put ever so perilously on hold.

But what would readily kill any tree, will bring only partial damage to a yew, especially *this* yew. So, she does not die. On the contrary, she is reawakened to life by the noises, mishaps and blunders of a clumsy visitor: the hermit.

Until then, humans had not really interfered with her woods. She could have listened to the alarming reports, broadcast by the subterranean fungal network, of tree fellings throughout the Island. But, she did not. She was too taken with enjoying herself and life. This newly arrived visitor is little more than entertainment. And entertain her he does, through all the apparently absurd activities of a (exceedingly clumsy) religious zealot. She enjoys watching him live out of tune with nature and so very far from that God (a God to be found in a book, the Bible, *not* on mountain-tops, or streams, or in the woods) whose blessing he seeks in vain. Autumn sets in.

When spring is sprung, there are two surprises. The hermit now resides within the yewess herself (he has built a tree house on top of her).[15] More crucially, there is nothing clumsy about him anymore. He looks and feels at perfect ease in the woods; his face is aglow with serenity.

The epiphany comes when he deliberately drinks a yew leaves' brew, and eats a handful of her arils, swallowing the stones too. That would be enough to kill a horse. But not *this* man. He tells her, "I know you can hear me. But I can hear you too."

Later on, she will notice leaves growing on the hermit's face, until his whole body will be covered with them. Eventually, we will realise that she has been hosting... the Green Man.

It struck me as a clever way to blend myth and lore with contemporary scientific, or rather post-scientific, theories. Much later in the narrative I will return to this subject, so this is a preview. What happened here, in a few words, is that the morphic field of the hermit *spilled over into that of the yewess*. This is out of Rupert Sheldrake's *A new Science of Life—The Hypothesis of Formative Causation*. That is how, as an outstanding exception, a man could communicate directly with a higher organism, the yew.

SEVEN

I have attempted to instil my story with an universality parallel to that of the yew tree itself. And, as every chapter is in itself a parable whose meaning touches us all, trees, animals, bacteria, cells, atoms, I felt I could not omit a topic which is part of life as much as it is coeval with it: conflict and outright war. From a narrow botanical standpoint, the tremendous

---

[15] I was inspired by the ancient Irish poem *The Hermit's Song*. I can't read Irish, but I was able to secure a few translations into English. My favourite one is Frank O' Connor's, which I adopted.

amount of competition and conflict carried out by trees in a forest has certainly demythologised bucolic peace. Indeed, war belongs also in the vegetable kingdom.[16]

Little did our yewess know that one day she would have to wage a full-fledged war against the yews' archenemy: the oaks. The Green Man's episode, although far more significant than it might appear at first sight, was an interlude. Now that her mother is no more, now that the oaks have taken advantage of more than thirty years of lack of leadership by invading much of the territory, it is high time to counterattack. But before doing so, she has to accept full responsibility and succeed to her mother as Queen of the Forest and of the Island.

Which she does *reluctantly*. At last, she *will* lead the evergreen trees into war.

I drew inspiration for the war tactics from a Chinese classic, the over two thousand-year-old *The Art of War (Sunzi bingfa / Sun-tzu ping-fa)*, compiled by the mysterious warrior/theoretician Sun Tzu. So as to prepare this mix, I blended strategic elements from one source, botanical from another, and elements of contemporary circumstantial evidence[17], plus my imagination, to create a cohesive narrative spanning over three centuries.

The war will last this long, and in the end the yewess will search within herself to find clues as to how to bring it to an end. She will then realise the lethal potential of her congenital chemical warfare capacities and put them to use. Indeed, she will overdo it.[18]

---

[16] "Allelopathy" is the botanical term that describes the inhibition and/or suppression of growth in one species of plants by toxins produced by the same or another species. Several types of plant hormones (internal and in this case external regulatory substances) exist and are utilised by plants. Among these auxin, which regulates various functions, including cell elongation; gibberellin, which promotes stem elongation; kinetin, which promotes cell division; and others. And to think that most countries have put a ban on chemical warfare...

[17] One above them all: the anomaly of the Killarney National Park Yew Wood. It is one of only three such pure stands of exclusively yew trees. Nature does not quite tolerate pure yew stands, as it does, for instance, with oak, beech, mango groves, etc. The Killarney Yew Stand is the biggest in the world, comprising the territory that lies astride Lower Lake and Middle Lake. Most of the native oaks are to be found across the peninsula in compact groves, almost suggesting that they have been pushed over there somehow (this is what I call "circumstantial evidence"). I could not resist the temptation to explain how the yew wood originated. I also explained that other oddity: the absence of woodpeckers in Ireland.

[18] Mycorrhizal fungi live in symbiosis with the non-woody, absorbing roots of the oaks. Many trees are dependent on this mutually beneficial fungus-root association, and the oaks particularly so, while yews can do with and without it, indifferently. In essence, a delicate balance between host plant, in this instance the oaks, and symbiont, the mycorrhizal fungi, results in enhanced mineral absorption for each member.

At the time of the oaks' root shedding, the yewess managed to discourage the formation of the root protection at the base of the dying roots. Without such a protection, the friend of yesterday became the foe of today. The fungi turned on the oak trees and began to digest the non-woody roots. The oaks put up a desperate fight, but in vain.

By the end of the war, having reached and, in perfect health and strengthened power, crossed the threshold of a thousand years of age, she will be victorious, and yet feel embittered and lonely.

EIGHT

In a 1904 ten-volume "edition de luxe" collection of Irish Literature, I chanced on a poem, *The Angel's Whisper,* by Samuel Lover which he himself, a great admirer of folklore as well as a practiced songwriter, must have read or heard somewhere else. Its first two strophes read:

> A baby was sleeping, its mother was weeping,
> For her husband was far on the wild raging sea,
> And the tempest was swelling, round the fisherman's dwelling,
> And she cried, "Dermot, darling, oh! come back to me."
>
> Her beads while she numbered, the baby still slumbered,
> And smiled in her face as she bended her knee;
> "Oh! blest be that warning, my child, thy sleep adorning,
> For I know that the angels are whispering with thee."

I envisioned a gnarled female yew tree—who narrated the tale to our yewess—by the door of the cottage (the "fisherman's dwelling"); I imagined the mother's prayers being granted; I continued with the fisherman's safe return, though his boat is no more; and then, under the influence of all of the above and of the haunting notes of *Fisherman's Blues,* by the Waterboys, I set the little cottage on the cliff ablaze with passion.

On the wings of love and analogy, I flew to Dunloe Castle, close to Killarney. There grow two magnificent yews, a female and a male specimen of at least half a millennium. I focused on their luxuriant foliage intertwined, intermingled, for centuries embraced, above ground as well as underground. I told of the pollen that the wind would blow from the male a few yards, feet, or at times just inches across to the female, ready to accept it so as to be impregnated and issue offspring shortly before autumn. Every year, since before the discovery of America.[19]

My yewess yearns for the same embrace, the same palpable affection, as she feels respected, but not loved. Blasphemy! one may exclaim. The yew tree, the Sacred Tree, the Tree of Knowledge, no less, mixed up with earthly desires. But who more than the yewess is a daughter of the earth?

---

[19] Many are the texts on plant sexology, with Charles Allen's *The Sexual Relations of Plants,* published in 1886, being the... seminal book.

Even humans, occasionally, are able to rise above mating and *make love*. Think about this inflated expression anew: to *make*, to *create*, *love*, no less. Sheer beauty. The yewess happens to witness nights of passion between a local princess and a monk from Innisfallen, an island in the midst of Lower Lake where a monastery was founded in the Seventh Century. The lovemaking between the two is of the incendiary type, and there is no way to extinguish such a flame other than with more fire. Lucretius comes to my rescue: *"Namque in eo spes est, unde est ardoris origo, restingui quoque posse ab eodem corpore flammam."* (For here lies the hope that the fire may be extinguished from the same body that was the origin of the burning, which nature contrariwise denies out and out to be possible.)[20] But the lovers don't care, as their love burns through the night, in the immediate vicinity of our tree. When it is time to part their ways, knowing this has been their last encounter, the passionate princess tells her lover: "Love all that is lovely;" (echoing W.B. Yeats; to which I add:) "love all you can and more than you can."

For ages the yewess had preferred certain clouds of pollen coming to her from a yew tree upwind from her, far afield. Never was she able to behold him. Yet, she longs to be beside him. So much so that she comes to desire what is impossible: to be "gravitationally unbound" (a jargony expression transplanted from the journal of science *Nature*, but more at home here). The heresy surfaces: she wants to *fly*, fly to her lover. But aren't there other great heresies in nature? Flightless birds and mammals who live like fish in the vast expanse of the salt-sea ocean?

So, those who *can* love, provided this love be genuine, *should* by all means love, and "love without restraint as young lovers do, for love dwells in everyone, and the lover is in you."

---

[20] And how appropriate it seems to insert, here, the counterpoint of some verses from that not at all dispassionate poet, but rather more passionate than most: Catullus, when chanting to his lover/life-long-obsession Lesbia:

Da mi basia mille, deinde centum,	*Give me a thousand kisses and a hundred more,*
dein mille altera, dein secunda centum,	*give me another thousand of them and a hundred more,*
deinde usque altera mille, deinde centum.	*always, always a thousand and then a hundred more.*
Dein, cum milia multa fecerimus,	*And when in the end there will be thousands of them,*
conturbabimus illa, ne sciamus,	*we'll entangle their account so as to forget everything,*
aut ne quis malus invidere possit,	*so that nobody may cast in an envious spell*
cum tantum sciat esse basiorum	*so great a number of kisses.*

NINE

Mister Hood was a gentle man
Always inspired by the sun,
But his real name was Herringbone,
His real name was Herringbone.

Thus begins a song I must have heard one time too many during my teens. I thought it might be fun to rewrite history, or reinterpret it once more, and point to Ireland as the birthplace of Robin Hood. I had read of one Ben of the Hills, after all, who did in Ireland exactly what his more famous peer did in England. Here was one more universal theme. And, of course, there would have been no Ben of the Hills, no Robin Hood, and no Herringbone, without the yew tree, from whose wood the famous longbows were made.

This is a sunny chapter. Though it can rain torrentially in the West of Ireland, and seemingly forever, I must keep to the brightness that pertains to Herringbone.

Who is Herringbone? A wretched, forsaken bastard, a beggar, but of a sunny, cheerful disposition in face of the giant adversity his life has always been. Until his encounter with the yewess, that is. She subliminally influences him and manages to make him tear off one of her branches. Such a branch will become a mighty longbow, whose morphic resonance will allow the yewess to keep track, at a distance, of Herringbone's adventures. Or rather misadventures, at first.

With time, he will become skilful in the art of archery and of stealing money to give back to the poor, as well as in the art of loving. Women will fantasise about kissing him above a mantle of wildflowers; sheriffs will be obsessed by the desire to capture him. Eventually, he will narrowly escape an ambush and cross the channel, landing on the bigger Island, to the east of Ireland. There his deeds will turn into an enterprise for the redistribution of wealth, with many merry bowmen joining him. But the longbow's signal, due to increased distance in both space and time, will blur and fade so that this lore will have to be sought elsewhere, says the yewess.

Once more, the theme of rebellion against injustice, rebellion against a destiny that no one but other men had laid out for Herringbone till he discovered he could alter it, and all thanks to "a wooden stick!"

TEN

The yewess comes of age, as her long-dormant innate memory comes into focus. She has already experienced the thrill of travelling, without moving, through kindred species (such as the Podocarpus, the Juniper, etc.) in a line of botanical proximity.[21] Now she realises that she can travel back in time thanks to her immense memory, her *collective consciousness*. She will go back to the first yew—*the first tree on this planet*. She will then see the dinosaurs, and their end, and then the whole evolution up to these uncouth newcomers: humans. She will see them terrorised and helpless at the mercy of beasts and natural phenomena. And she will wonder at Mother Nature's own imperfections. Why would she engineer such unperfectible animals as the dinosaurs? Why would she have man come about, her worst error? For surely man, at his initial stage of scarce cerebral syntax, is less fit than many other mammals.[22] But he, unlike the dinosaurs, is perfectible. Alarmingly so. Man will master nature, but will soon make it manifest that he cannot control his plundering and murderous inclinations.

Her biological mother had died, making it clear that death eventually befalls even a yew tree. Her sterner, natural mother, Mother Nature, was beginning to come under her scrutiny, and many flaws were to be found in her doings. The yewess might feel forsaken, but she is too involved in her time travel, too self-conceited to be bothered by nature's inherent unfairness.

---

[21] This is elaborated, albeit quite indirectly, from Rupert Sheldrake's theories. When telling him viva voce about the yewess's global interconnectedness via a line of direct botanical proximity, it struck him as a clever and plausible idea within the context of his beliefs. Until reading his works, I was persuaded—or had been persuaded—that, after the historical divorce between science and religion(s), we lived in a scientific/technological priesthood in which everything could be accounted for from a mere mechanistic perspective. Sheldrake made me realise that even a scientist could have spiritual leanings, and believe in something other than what our puny measuring instruments could record. The microscope and telescope, to name but two instruments, have shown us quite dramatically that, indeed, "there is more than meets the eye". The visible world has ever been governed by the invisible world. In spite of this, Western science requires palpable proof for everything it proposes. Yet, determinism was superseded by Heisenberg over seventy years ago. And Euclidean geometry over a century ago. As for logics (the last, hard-to-die legacy of positivism), they were disembowelled and unwittingly brought to an end by Lukasiewicz's multivalued calculi / many-valued logic.

The world needs scientists attuned to many realities, mindful that man is embedded in his environment and traditions. In other words, Sheldrake's influence on my work does not stem from an inclination towards erudition or eccentricity. Rather, it derives from a necessity to put the spirit back into this world, where it belongs.

Another pertinent instance of compatibility between science and the spirit is represented by Sir Ghillean Prance, himself a great admirer of *The Story of Yew*. A quasi-legendary ethnobotanist, and a world-class scientist, he is a deeply religious man.

[22] See the striking passage in Lucretius's *De Rerum Natura,* Book 5, 925-1010.

ELEVEN

Some Franciscan friars settle in her forest and decide to build an abbey [1448]. Quite "unfranciscanly", they start clearing the woods so as to obtain an unobstructed view of the lake. The first illustrious victim is the Queen of the Forest!

It is of course ironic that the axmen, i.e., the *profaners*, are friars. That is a shortcoming of the Christian religion: its neglect of nature, its utter anthropocentrism. I cannot help surmising that this is due to the place of origin of Christianity, and before that of Judaism: barren, arid—shall I say, "gardening-unfriendly"?—hills and deserts characterised by strong sunlight but very scarce rainfall. The divinities of the Celtic religions were immensely more attuned to the surrounding nature, probably because *there was much verdant nature to be attuned to*. The most sacrilegious act, therefore, is carried out quite light-heartedly by the delegates of the religion imported by Patrick a thousand years before.

Her "resurrection", though scientifically accounted for and plausible[23], reeks of something miraculous, and that is why she is suddenly spared and preserved. The very friars responsible for her felling, noticing twelve sprouts coming back from her severed trunk, see in them the twelve apostles and the central message of the resurrection of Christ, and decide to build the cloister round her stump, rather than remove it.

It is only now, wounded almost to death, humiliated, violated, raped, that she pays attention to all the suffering that has occurred on her Island. Only now, paradoxically, does she become her Island's caring Queen, now that she at last hears and feels the cries of agony of millions of trees felled by human hands.

If at first hate may be the prime force that jolts her back into life, with time and with deeper understanding—compassion—she will stay alive for the opposite reason: love.

TWELVE

The yewess by now calls the humans "kind listeners"! After having scorned them for centuries and thought of them as lowly beasts. She does not care to insult anybody or anything anymore. For the sake of the few innocent humans there might be, she produces a list of the atrocities and devastation her Island had to suffer through the wrongdoing of man.

Ireland (as the invaded) much more so than England (as the invader) symbolises the plight of deforestation all the way to the extreme of desertification. Eire was a *woodland*; the English, in the shipbuilding craze that fed their maritime empire, turned it into a *grassland*. If she has not

---

[23] Regeneration by epicormic sprouts, sustained by the energy stored in the roots' cells.

become a desert, it is thanks to the mixed blessings of her abundant rainfall.

There is something universal in the plight of the invaded, the usurped, the aggressed, the wounded, the murdered. Nearly every nation on Earth, in its history, has known the pain of being taken hostage in its own land. Some nations have had this dismal experience many times. For others, it was a nightmare lasting centuries. If for one moment you substitute a virus for an invading army, an illness for a war, then you come up with a universal reality that is simply, and unfortunately, part of life, as we know it, everywhere, at any time.

But hope must *never* die. We must stare at life's implicit, disconcerting ambivalence. It is our duty to tilt the balance, if a balance it is at all, between good and evil. Despite the callousness of the invaders and their widespread brutality, despite famine and mass evictions, there are a few hopeful signs of man finally coming to his senses, though not before the beginning of our century. They come to the yewess through the mouth of a charming little French girl, Claire, whom she calls "blessed little herald of truth". Some more tangible signs will follow, such as the inaugurations of the first national parks, wildlife reserves and, this expression being my favourite, even "natural sanctuaries".

A few lifesavers struggling in the midst of a raging sea, but something to hang on to, anyhow.

THIRTEEN

The yewess, by now two thousand years old, has lived a grand, rich, victorious life. She has overcome all odds, including being cut down to the ground. Once more she can declare to the world her sovereignty. She has been made a national monument, with a protective iron railing round her trunk; explanatory plaques on the abbey walls; and regular check-ups from the deputy superintendent of the National Park, on the direct instructions of the Office of Public Works.[24]

A greener yewess would have felt hugely proud. She would have found, in her triumph, cause for celebration. But she now knows better.

She has been given a voice, and decided to reach down to us. She has seen it all, far more than she cares to divulge. There is no tolerance for injustice. She cares no longer for Mother Nature, which she perceives as an unkind, harsh mother. She accuses "natural selection", for nothing so abominably unfair as the survival of the fittest should ever have been defined as "natural", but rather, with all its cruelty, *unnatural*.[25] She has

---

[24] The real-life Muckross Abbey Yew was the subject of some delighted comments by W. M. Thackerary in his 1842 *The Irish Sketch Book*. Previously, Thomas Crofton Croker, in his *Killarney Legends,* had devoted a section of Chapter V, entitled *The Abbey*, to the Yew.

lived a wonderful life, hasn't she? She ought to be most grateful, and thank mother nature for such a privilege. But what about all those organisms who cannot even claim to have lived a *decent* life, let alone wonderful?

Mother nature could kill her for such a heresy and for her lack of gratitude. Well, Go ahead, she dares her, defiantly. Or, if only for a moment, try to imagine a kindlier place—destitute of competition, competitors, where every grain of pollen pollinates a flower, where there is room to roam for everyone...

Humans should not believe that the world is governed by eternal laws. There are only habits, and the inertia set in motion by force of habit.

She is by now an all-loving creature, and loves everyone, everything unconditionally. She has more than forgiven all the wrongdoers—she loves them without reservation. But such an unconditional love is not tenable in the harsh vegetable kingdom. It is time, therefore, that she set off on a pathway of deliverance. Perhaps, she hopes, if we all thought about that strifeless place of unlimited bounty, then it might come into being. Perhaps, it already exists.

And, consciously, she lets go. "There are now only five leaves left."[26] (Rendered with five blank pages in the book.) "When you will have unhurriedly turned over the last leaf, it will have dawned once more and I will have issued forth, skyward, aloft and yonder."

Having said this, we have now come full circle, back to Wittgenstein's: "About that of which we cannot speak, we must remain silent."

---

[25] Certain all too absolutistic aspects of Darwinism have been exposed by the work of scientists involved in the science of Complexity. Even Neo-Darwinism is becoming obsolete, and it fosters, and certainly has fostered, pernicious persuasions and relative acts on the part of people and governments attempting to assert their superiority over other peoples. Evolution is yet another myth fabricated by the scientific priesthood that urgently needs reappraisal.

[26] *Five Leaves Left* is the title of a legendary album by the English folk singer Nick Drake.

The Muckross Abbey Yew in Killarney National Park,
County Kerry, Eire

Acknowledgements

One of the maxims of modernity prescribes: "Everybody is important, but nobody is indispensable." Quite to the contrary, many if not all those whom I thank in the following lines have proved indispensable in their contribution to *The Story of Yew*, be they humans, places, or trees. Indeed, without them this project would have not been possible.

I am unreservedly thankful to you, Stenie, for all your support. Unlike most (congenial) wives, you've proved once more to be not just delightful, but inspirational in my rendition of a female character. Then our sons. Tano created the dialogue between father and daughter in Chapter Twelve; Pietro kept me down to earth with hundreds of interruptions, but I could never bring myself to lock the door; Nicky was actually born halfway through the writing of the memoirs. Thank you all.

To the late Alan Mitchell, Victoria Medal of Honour, Trustee of the Tree Register of the British Isles, I express my gratitude for his inestimable botanical help; his generosity; and his friendship, born out of a common love of trees and knowledge. His dependable encouragement, dozens of closely typed letters, telephone conversations, meetings and meals together were more than inspiring—they were essential. The world has lost a great man. My gratitude goes also to his wife Philippa, herself knowledgeable and generous.

To the late Mr. Aidan Brady, Director of the National Botanic Gardens, at Glasnevin, Dublin, I address the same gratefulness which, luckily, I was able to manifest to him when he was still with us. His contribution has been of the utmost importance.

Sir Ghillean Prance: thank you for your unceasing support; for reading the manuscript in its various incarnations; for your suggestions; and for your marvellous friendship.

Rupert Sheldrake: thank you for your intelligence and your friendship. Thank you also for your hypotheses and theories, some aspects of which I have incorporated in the novel.

Jill Purce: thank you for your acumen, helpfulness, and influence in the higher spheres.

Christopher Sinclair-Stevenson: thank you for your "transverse" editing, your many suggestions, and characteristic patience.

My gratefulness for their warm endorsement and support to:

The Conservation Foundation, which began its campaign for greater awareness of the UK's ancient yew trees in 1987. Through a variety of magazine articles and radio and television features the Foundation encouraged people to measure old yew trees so that estimates of their ages could be recorded on certificates to display in nearby churches and public buildings. 10 years later the Foundation launched its unique Yews for the Millennium initiative whereby it invited local communities to celebrate the year 2000 by planting young trees taken as cuttings from almost 40 yews estimated to be at least 2000 years old. Almost 8000 yews have since been distributed and many of those planting trees have now begun an on-going association with the Foundation as Parish Pumps enabling them to receive environmental information and advice to pass on to their local communities. The Yews for the Millennium team: Prof David Bellamy, David Shreeve, Libby Symon, Charlotte Triggs, Fergus Kinmonth (collector of cuttings), Martin Day (grower of cuttings).

Dr Stephen Blackmore; the Natural History Museum and Royal Botanic Garden Edinburgh.

Professor Richard Bateman, Keeper of Botany at the the Natural History Museum.

Jean-Paul Jeanrenaud of WWF, both UK and International; one of the first to offer his contribution and help, both with fraternal generosity and superior competence.

Ivan Hattingh, Director of Development, for his support and creative promotion, at WWF UK.

The Royal Botanic Gardens at Kew.

Robert Osborne, and The Tree Council.

John Caunce and Lt Col Carr, and the International Tree Foundation.

Martin Blunt, and Tree Spirit.

The late Phil Drabble.

Pini Araldi Guinetti, lover of belles lettres and good friend: thank you for years of understanding, support, and epitostolary exchanges. Last but not least, thank you very much for your generosity.

Much gratitude to the Department of Arts, Heritage, Gaeltacht and the Islands; its minister, Síle de Valera, T.D.; her personal secretary, Sheila Clifford; and the wonderful Frank McGeough.

My thanks to Mr. Donal Synnot, then helpful Curator of the Herbarium at Glasnevin, now Director of the National Botanic Gardens, Glasnevin. A wonderful outdoors lecturer and a kind and meticulous assistant to my endeavour.

Mr. Cormac Foley, former Deputy Superintendent of the Killarney National Park, Co. Kerry: thank you so much for introducing me to all the yews who wound up telling their Story. All your escorting *in loco* and your correspondence before and after my visits have been absolutely priceless. You showed me, however unwittingly, that the story had written itself.

Mr. Danny Cronin, former Overseer of the Killarney National Park; Council Member (as well as founder) of The Irish Deer Society, and fabulous story-teller: thank you for your tales, details and words of wisdom.

Dan Kelleher, Regional Manager; and Paddy O'Connor, Office Supervisor, Killarney National Park.

Allen Meredith, thank you. We have both heard the cry of the yew. As George Macdonald would have it:

"Thou goest thine, and I'll go mine — Many ways we wend; / Many days, and many ways, Ending in one end. / Many a wrong, and its curing song; / Many a road, and many an inn; / Room to roam, but only one home / For all the world to win."

Dr. Alex Shigo: thank you for your suggestions and for your convincingly (and vehemently substantiated!) revolutionary outlook on things green.

Marco Salvi: thank you for years of encouragement and support, for your generous hospitality from Westwood (Los Angeles) to Chelsea (London), and for consitently being present when it matters.

Federico Mennella: thank you for years of care, support, encouragement, and for helping this specific project.

Gardner Monks, littérateur, bibliophile, cinema wizard, and true friend: thank you for your thoughtful insights; your support and patience; and your consistent willingness to help.

Elisabeth Wansbrough: thank you for your appreciation and incitement.

Jonathan Williams, thank you for all things Irish.

Grant & Joyce Beglarian, Bob Silverstein, Gabriele Vugliano (in memoriam), and Dado Redaelli Sommi Picinardi: thank you all for your marvellous encouragement.

Thanks also to Ms. Julia Hickey, Assistant Librarian at the Natural History Museum, London; Miss C A Oldham of the Forestry Commission Library; Mrs. Barbara V Lowry, Administrative Officer at the Library of the Royal Botanic Gardens, Kew.

Emma Cummings, and the stupendous Eden Project.

Ernesto (Pescini): thank you for sharing your art.

Thierry and Karin, Sue, Carol and all at Findhorn Press on both sides of the Atlantic: bravi, and thank you. And thank you, Tony Mitton, for your marvellous *labor limae* and suggestions.

In Chapter Thirteen I touch lightly and quite disapprovingly, I'm afraid, on a wondrous human project: "Bringing Mars to Life". It has been propounded in an article published on the journal of science *Nature*

(Volume 352; No. 6335) and authored by: Christopher P McKay, Owen B Toon & James F Kasting.

The ancient Irish poem from which I quote a few passages in Chapter Six, *The Hermit's Song*, has been translated into English by Frank O'Connor.

Ireland and her people have been an inspiration in themselves, so thank you, green and visionary Island, thank you, green and visionary people.

The venerable Muckross Abbey Yew is the *conditio sine qua non* of the entire project; words cannot thank this tree enough.

Lastly, thank yew and you, Trees, all of you, as many as in the very many species. You have put up with us since we first appeared on Earth, the victims of our careless rites. Now you have been voiced. Who knows? In all hopefulness, we shall have new rites, kindlier rites.

But all who read, beware. All parts of the yew, leaves, twigs, bark and wood are toxic, except the berries (technically called "arils"). Indeed, they are lethal for us humans and for most animals. But the berries are perfectly edible, though one must take the all important precaution NOT to ingest the pip they contain, which, particularly if crunched, is also poisonous. If you choose to eat the berry, you MUST discard the pip first.

Notes

Notes

Notes

Notes

Notes

Notes

Notes

FINDHORN
Press

Findhorn Press is the publishing business of the Findhorn Community which has grown around the Findhorn Foundation in northern Scotland.

For further information about the Findhorn Foundation and the Findhorn Community, please contact:

Findhorn Foundation
The Visitors Centre
The Park, Findhorn IV36 3TY, Scotland, UK
tel 01309 690311• fax 01309 691301
email reception@findhorn.org
www.findhorn.org

For a complete Findhorn Press catalogue, please contact:

Findhorn Press

The Park, Findhorn,   P. O. Box 13939
Forres IV36 3TY   Tallahassee
Scotland, UK   Florida 32317-3939, USA
Tel 01309 690582   Tel (850) 893 2920
freephone 0800-389-9395   toll-free 1-877-390-4425
Fax 01309 690036   Fax (850) 893 3442
e-mail info@findhornpress.com
http://www.findhornpress.com